I0797775

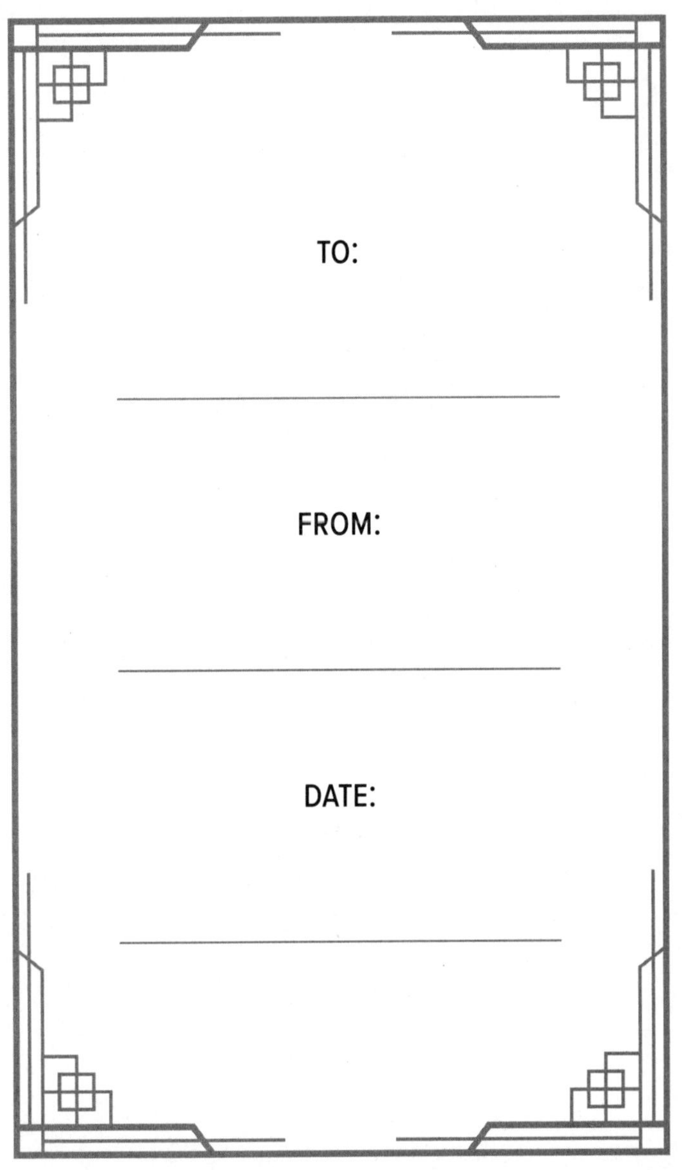

TO:

FROM:

DATE:

TO:

FROM:

DATE:

Finding PEACE IN THE PSALMS

100 DEVOTIONS TO
RESTORE YOUR SOUL

RAY PRITCHARD

Christian Art
PUBLISHERS

Visit Christian Art Gifts, Inc., at www.christianartgifts.com.

Finding Peace in the Psalms: 100 Devotions to Restore Your Soul

Previously published by Moody Publishers under the title *Green Pastures, Quiet Waters: Refreshing Moments from the Psalms.* Copyright © 1999. Revised and updated.

Published by Christian Art Gifts, Inc., Bloomingdale, IL, USA.

First edition 2025.

Designed by Christian Art Gifts, Inc.

Cover and interior images used under license from Shutterstock.com.

Most Christian Art titles may be purchased at bulk discounts by churches, nonprofits, and corporations. For more information, please email SpecialMarkets@cagifts.com.

ISBN 978-1-63952-903-2

Printed in China.

30 29 28 27 26 25
10 9 8 7 6 5 4 3 2 1

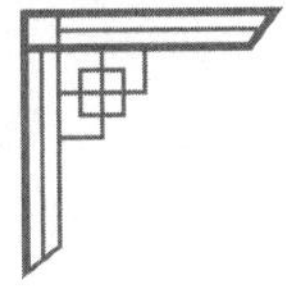
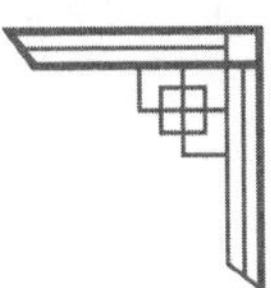

Dedicated with joy to

Alan and Donna Pritchard

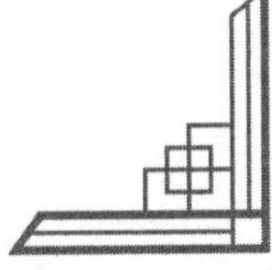

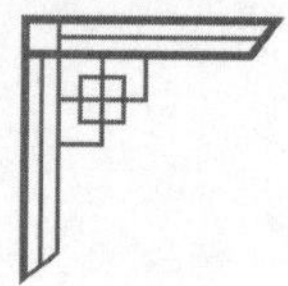
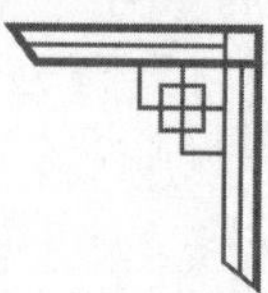

O magnify the Lord *with me,*
and let us exalt His name together.

PSALM 34:3 (KJV)

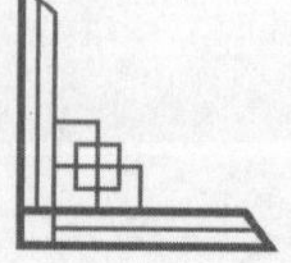
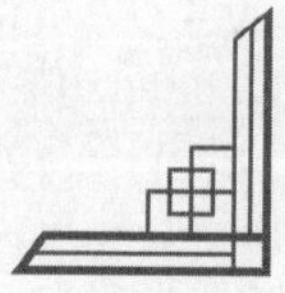

CONTENTS

INTRODUCTION

The book of Psalms is #1.

You don't have to take my word for it. A recent survey on Bible Gateway confirmed that fact.

It's easy to see why people love the Psalms. Across the centuries, stretching back thousands of years, people of faith have turned to these ancient hymns for hope, encouragement, direction, and inspiration.

The green pastures and quiet waters of the twenty-third Psalm are familiar to Christians and unbelievers alike. Few have been disappointed in this book of Scripture because the Psalms are—as Calvin has said—an anatomy of every part of the soul.

Whether you are happy or sad, defeated or triumphant, seeking wisdom or simply needing to pour out your soul to God, there is something here for you.

Many years ago, I heard a missionary say he liked to take "a morning dip in the Psalms." The image of a man swimming in the cool waters has stayed in my mind as a way to understand why this part of the Bible remains so popular.

Leviticus is the Word of God too, and so is Nahum, and 2 Peter for that matter. However, I don't know anyone who habitually reads those books every morning. But many Christians read the Psalms every day. Some read five a day so they can finish the book in a month and thus read it through twelve times a year.

Some people read the Psalms dozens of times, and a few people read it hundreds of times. Surely there must be something special about a book that never loses its hold over people. It speaks to the human condition because, although the world of David (who wrote many of the psalms) is long gone, the needs of the heart have not changed.

We all desperately need the Lord, and we need Him more than we know.

When you read Psalm 23 for the fiftieth time, you find it just as refreshing as the first time you discovered that "The Lord is my shepherd; I shall not want" (KJV).

The book you are holding in your hand is not a commentary on the Psalms. It's too short to be a commentary, and I'm not qualified to write one. To borrow a phrase, here you have one hundred morning dips in the Psalms.

I want to take you on a journey into every part of the Psalter. Since there are 150 psalms, I can't cover all of them, or even every verse in each psalm that we will visit. This book is like a tour bus: We don't have time to see everything, but together we'll visit some of the more intriguing sites, and I'll offer some commentary on the passing scenery.

When we're done, I hope you'll return and visit the many nooks and crannies of Psalms left untouched.

I've included a short prayer with each entry to guide your response to God. You'll also find questions to help you go deeper.

As we begin, let's remember that the book of Psalms is first and foremost a hymnbook for the people of God. If we read it without responding in praise, prayer, worship, and confession, then we've missed the reason this book is in the Bible.

One final word: I hope you won't read this book straight through. It's meant to be picked up and read a little bit at a time—an entry here, an entry there, perhaps two or three entries at a time.

If you feel like stopping to sing or to pray or to jot down

some notes, put this book aside and spend some time with the Lord. If you want to skip around in the book, that's fine too.

My only goal is to lead you into Psalms in a new way and ultimately for you to meet the One about Whom every psalm speaks.

If you're ready for an adventure in the Psalms, turn the page and let's get started.

HOW TO GET STARTED RIGHT

He is like a tree planted
by streams of water,
which yields its fruit in season
and whose leaf does not wither.
Whatever he does prospers.

PSALM 1:3

Would you like to be blessed by God every day?

Psalm 1 tells us how blessing happens, so let's pay attention to God's recipe for success. As we study this psalm, we discover that blessedness relates to the way we live and the choices we make. It depends on the kind of people we are. From God's point of view, there are only two ways to live because there are two kinds of people in the world and only two kinds. There are the righteous, and then there are the wicked. Everyone in the world falls into those two categories. There is no "in-between" category. Psalm 1 shows us how the righteous live and why they are blessed. It also shows us the result of both ways of life.

Psalm 1 surprises many people because it begins not with the positive but with a negative. *The blessing begins with what the righteous person does not do.*

He does not walk in the counsel of the wicked.
He does not stand in the way of sinners.
He does not sit in the seat of mockers.

Blessings come not only from what we do, but also from what we don't do. Blessed people avoid certain things. And they avoid certain people and certain situations. They don't hang out just anywhere and they don't quickly buy into every line of thinking. They are very careful not to join themselves to the company of those who do not love the Lord.

Now we come to the positive side of the ledger. Having refused to walk in the way of evildoers, we instead focus on knowing God's Word. We do this because the best way to float rubbish out is to pour water in. You can't eliminate the garbage in your life simply by mental effort. You must replace the negative with something positive. The psalmist tells us the godly person "delights" in the law of the Lord. That means he loves the Word of God, the Holy Scriptures, the Bible. The word *delight* means to take great pleasure in. It has the idea of a consuming passion that controls your life.

Everyone "delights" in something. Some people delight in food. Others delight in a job or a hobby or a career. Some delight in a particular friendship. Many people delight in money, or the things money can buy. And many delight in evil pleasures and wrong desires. Mark this well. *Your delight determines your direction.*

The happiest people in the world are those whose lives are built on the Word of God. We can state that more forcefully. *The only truly happy people in the world are those who follow the prescription of Psalm 1.* Others may be happy in a temporary or worldly sense, but they do not know the joy and deep satisfaction that comes from living with God's approval. That is reserved for the true children of God.

A blessing awaits those who build their lives upon this ancient book. May that blessing be ours so that we, having been blessed, may be a blessing to others in the year to come.

Lord Jesus, in these momentous days,
when the world shakes beneath our feet,
help us to be people of the Word, delighting
in what You have given us. Amen.

1. What are some ways we are tempted to "walk in the way of the wicked"?
2. What does it mean to say that your "delight determines your direction"?
3. How can you enter into the blessing promised in Psalm 1?

GOD'S FOREIGN POLICY

Why do the nations conspire
and the peoples plot in vain?
PSALM 2:1

Does God have a foreign policy?
The answer may surprise you.

The Bible says much about the nations of the world—their origin, their alliances, their political power, their military might, their ultimate destiny. It reminds us again and again that the nations derive their strength from God and that without Him, they are nothing. They are like a drop of water in a full bucket to Him (Isa. 40:15).

That raises an interesting question: Does God have a foreign policy? The answer is yes. Does God care what the nations do? Yes. Does He pay attention to world leaders? Yes. Does He take their threats seriously? Yes. Psalm 2 shows us God's foreign policy. In the face of world-wide rebellion against the Lord, God declares His intention to someday enthrone Christ as ruler over the nations of the world. The only proper response to His coming reign is humble submission to Him right now. The first few verses remind us that the world has always been an enemy of God. The nations "rage" (KJV), the rulers "plot in vain," planning their attack on the Almighty, who scoffs at their puny plans.

He answers them by installing His Son as King over the entire earth. Someday all the nations will bow in submission before Jesus Christ. Philippians 2:9–11 echoes this truth with its promise that "every knee should bow … and every tongue confess that Jesus Christ is Lord, to the glory of God the Father."

Meanwhile God invites world rulers to "kiss the Son"—to bow in humble submission at His feet. Rebels will be judged, but God's children will be kept safe in the Day of Judgment.

Every nation will eventually bow before Jesus Christ the King. This gives us great confidence when we pray. Since man left to himself always turns away from God, we should not be surprised to find ourselves in a minority position in society. Although we ought to do what we can to improve the world, we must not put our final trust in politicians or political parties.

Today the nations rage; tomorrow the King comes to judge them. Between now and then, "blessed are all who take refuge in Him" (v. 12).

Psalm 2 calls the church back to its central mission:

- Personal submission to Jesus as Lord.
- Proclamation of the gospel to every nation.
- Growing confidence in God amid chaos on earth.

Let's lift up Jesus as the only hope of the world. And let's invite the rebels to put down their weapons and join us in the great celebration of God's Son, the Anointed One, our coming King—Jesus Christ.

Omnipotent God, the nations are but a drop in the bucket to You. Open my eyes to see beyond the headlines to the hurting hearts in every land. Amen.

1. What evidence suggests that the rulers of the world "rage" against God and against His Son?
2. Why does God laugh when human rulers unite against Him?
3. Take a few moments to thank God that He sits enthroned above the chaos of the nations.

WORSHIP IS SERIOUS BUSINESS!

Serve the L*ORD* *with fear*
and rejoice with trembling.
PSALM 2:11

Are you ready for church?

That's a good question for today. I'm not asking if you are dressed and ready to go. I'm asking about your heart. Are you ready to worship God with fear and rejoicing? I wonder how many of us would answer "yes."

Rejoicing and trembling may seem like opposite emotions, but the psalmist joins them together as the proper way to approach God. We are to rejoice that we know the Lord, but we are never, ever to take Him lightly. As Charles Spurgeon says, this is a "sacred compound."

Fear without joy is torment, and joy without fear is presumption. Martin Luther pointed out that hypocrites rejoice in God without fear because they have too high an opinion of themselves. But the righteous despair of themselves, thus they tremble; casting themselves upon God, they rejoice in His mercy.

True believers constantly accuse themselves (in the sense of being deeply aware of their own sinfulness) and simultaneously rejoice in God their Savior. They are like wheat when the husk of self-trust is broken off, leaving only the sweet fruit of Christ within.

The word *trembling* carries with it the concept of timidity and fear—which might seem to contradict the invitation to "come boldly" to the throne of grace (Heb. 4:16 KJV). We are invited to come to God as often as we like—especially in the "time of need"—but we must not come lightly, flippantly, or casually.

We are to tremble in the presence of the Lord, to feel such gratitude for the awesome privilege of knowing Him that we come into His presence knowing we are standing before the King of the universe.

If that thought doesn't make you fearful, it should. It's the sudden fear that grips you late at night when you are almost asleep, right on the edge, and suddenly you hear a tiny noise, a strange sound, and you think: *Burglars have broken in*!

It happens to me from time to time. I'll be drifting off to sleep when I hear something creak. Suddenly I'm wide awake, sitting up in bed, straining to hear every sound. One writer called it "aroused fear in the moment of danger." Serve God that way so you can hear everything He is saying to you in the Word. It keeps you on your toes.

Worship is serious business. Don't take it lightly. Don't drift away from the Lord. Stay on your toes. Be alert. We know how easy it is to go to church and just tune out. We're there, but we're not there. We're looking attentive, but our mind is ten thousand miles away.

Let's take Psalm 2 to heart today. God wants our wholehearted worship—nothing less!

O God of all things, help me not to take lightly that which You take seriously. Amen.

1. Have you ever trembled over your own sin?
2. How can such self-despair lead to rejoicing?
3. What can we do to keep from taking God lightly?

KEEP COOL AND KEEP QUIET

In your anger do not sin; when you are on your beds, search your hearts and be silent.

PSALM 4:4

Here's some news you can use.
You don't have to say everything you're thinking.

That especially applies when you are tired and running low on patience. Be careful about what you say. Usually, you'll be happier if you say nothing at all.

Paul quoted the first part of this verse in Ephesians 4:26, adding this application: "Do not let the sun go down while you are still angry." The principle is easy to grasp: *Solving problems now saves trouble later*, and delayed reconciliation means increased animosity.

Not all anger is sinful, but anger is such a powerful emotion that when we fail to deal with it properly, it can quickly harden into malice, rage, or even murder (see Matt. 5:21–26). Dealing with anger righteously is more important than going to church; it's more important than giving money; it's more important than praying in public or attending a Bible study.

Jesus taught us that uncontrolled anger is really a form of murder in the heart. But you say, "I'm no murderer."

That's what you are if you harbor bitterness and resentment toward someone else. A murderer in church? How could that be? When anger fills your heart, you are prone to abusive speech because you harbor resentment toward others. Some Christians I know are so cruel in their speech that they leave a trail of bloody words wherever they go. God's message is clear: *Either you learn to control your anger, or your anger will destroy you from the inside out.*

Let me ask three questions that probe at a deep level:

- Do you find it easy to lose your temper when things don't go your way?
- Are you carrying a chip on your shoulder?
- Is your anger keeping you from reconciling with those who have hurt you?

We need a spiritual alarm within that begins to sound the moment anger takes over. "Ring! Ring! Ring! Danger! Murder Ahead!" Where anger prevails, murder cannot be far behind. Given the right circumstances, all of us would commit murder. Our hands are not clean because our lips are not clean.

Why bring this up? *Because we are guilty of the very thing we said we would never do.* We tend to be very quick to excuse ourselves.

Please understand that the Lord Jesus is not as quick to let us off the hook as we are. If we take Him seriously, then we've got to stop making excuses for our hidden anger, our buried resentments, and our tongue that is as sharp as a razor.

Don't bury your anger. Deal with it. Talk it out with a friend. Take it to the Lord in prayer. Don't go to bed angry, or you'll wake up with a short fuse.

Lord Jesus, when I am angry,
teach me to forgive as You forgave
those who sinned against You. Amen.

1. Consider the three questions in this entry.
2. Which ones are true of you right now?
3. What are you going to do about it?

DON'T GIVE UP ON GOD

In the morning, O Lord, you hear my voice;
in the morning I lay my requests before
you and wait in expectation.
PSALM 5:3

God wants us to believe in Him.

A speaker posed this question to his audience: "If you could ask God to do one thing for you in the spiritual realm, what would it be?" There is an endless list of possible answers to a question like that:

- Break a bad habit.
- Forgive someone who hurt me.
- Have my child come back to God.
- See my loved one come to Christ.
- Change my character.
- Know deliverance from discouragement.
- Have new zeal for God.
- Receive power to overcome temptation.
- Be bold for Christ.

Whatever it is, it's not too hard for God.

Each week members of my congregation submit prayer requests to the staff. Each Tuesday as I look at the list, I am struck by the many needs of our people. Some of the requests are truly heartbreaking. Yet as I consider the list, I want to write Genesis 18:14 at the top, "Is anything too hard for the LORD?" No matter how impossible your request may seem to you, it's not too hard for God.

I ran across this provocative statement: "The only thing that hinders God is our unbelief." We have to stop and think about that for a moment because it doesn't sound right to say anything "hinders" God. And in the literal sense, nothing does. He is the Sovereign Lord of the universe. No one can stand against Him.

Yet in His wisdom, He has ordained that He will limit His work in the world according to the faith of His people. In that sense, it is perfectly proper to say our faith or the lack of it either opens the door for the Almighty or "ties His hands," so to speak. Billy Graham has remarked that heaven is filled with answers for which no one bothered to ask:

- Are you willing to wait?
- Are you willing to work?
- Are you willing to believe God?

What do you believe deep in your heart? Is anything too hard for the Lord? Anything in your life so big that He can't handle it? You already know the answer is no, but I'm asking it differently. What problem seems so impossible that part of you doubts God can take care of it?

God wants us to believe in Him. He begs us to believe in Him. He dares us to trust Him.

Is your problem too hard for the Lord? If you answer yes, then what hope is left for you? But if you say no, then you will have a bright tomorrow! The choice is yours. Thousands upon thousands of times, many thousands of believers across the centuries have put God to the test. They have trusted Him, and He has come through for them.

What about you?

Are you willing to trust Him with your problems?

Eternal God, You are so much
bigger than my puny faith. I believe,
Lord—help Thou my unbelief. Amen.

1. What one thing would you like God to do for you?
2. Are you willing to wait for Him to work?
3. Write down your request, and then write Genesis 18:14 over it.

HEALING STARTS IN YOUR HEART

Be merciful to me, Lord, for I am faint;
O Lord, heal me, for my bones are in agony.
PSALM 6:2

This is the first of the penitential psalms.

It's a prayer born out of desperate circumstances. We don't know the precise circumstances behind David's prayer, but that doesn't matter because they speak to a universal need for forgiveness and healing of the mind, body, and soul.

Doctors have long known that there is a close relationship between the physical and spiritual sides of life. Although the precise relationship is difficult to define or quantify, every doctor has seen the principle in action. Ask any doctor and they will tell stories about patients who should have died but didn't—the only possible explanation was their positive, hope-filled outlook on life. Ask that same doctor and they will give you other stories of people who came into treatment in a negative or angry or hostile mode and who stayed sick longer than they should have.

When you approach life positively and with an optimistic outlook, you are much more likely to stay healthy. A negative attitude often leads to poor health. Solomon reflected this truth when he wrote that "a cheerful heart is good medicine, but a crushed spirit dries up the bones" (Prov. 17:22).

It is fascinating that James connected prayer for healing with confession of sin (James 5:14–16). He seems to imply that when the elders pray over the sick, they are to inquire as to the spiritual status of the sick person, which suggests the sickness might be connected with unresolved issues in the soul.

Over the decades of my ministry, I have seen this principle repeatedly. As the church leaders gather to pray for the sick, we always ask, "Are you aware of anything in your life that might be causing your current sickness?" Usually, the answer is negative, but occasionally, the person will respond with a confession that involves bitterness, unforgiveness, or other debilitating sins that can block God's healing power.

This is not to suggest all sickness is connected to personal sin. But sometimes it is, and when that happens, thoughtful Christians will encourage the person to take steps of confession, repentance, and where appropriate, restitution. In other cases, sickness exists not because of any particular sin but simply as a result of living in a sin-cursed world.

When Jesus comes back, sin and sickness will finally be banished from the earth forever. Until that day, us believers can demonstrate our faith amid sickness, and we also have the privilege of bringing our cases to the Great Physician and asking for the healing we need.

Lord Jesus, create in me a clean heart that
I might be healed from the inside out. Amen.

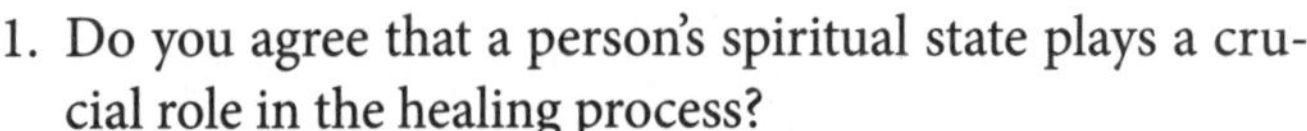

1. Do you agree that a person's spiritual state plays a crucial role in the healing process?
2. Have you ever seen anyone get better (or worse) because of this principle?
3. Why does healing almost always begin in the heart?

PRACTICAL WAYS TO PUT GOD FIRST

I will praise you,
O Lord, with all my heart;
I will tell of all your wonders.
PSALM 9:1

If Jesus is to be the Lord,
then worship must have priority.

Do you worship with all your heart? If we are honest, we will probably say, "It's hard in our family because there is so much going on." If worship is going to be important, then preparation for worship will become very important. Consider the typical Sunday morning routine. You get up, fix and eat breakfast, shave or put on your makeup, fix your hair, iron your clothes, put on your dress or your coat and tie, pile the kids in the car, and barely make it to the service.

How much time did you spend preparing your heart for the worship of God? You had to get your face ready—what about your heart? You had to iron your pants, but did you take time to iron the wrinkles out of your soul?

How do you think God feels when He paid the price of His Son's blood, and His people come in late and unprepared to worship Him?

Your attitude changes how you come to worship. When

your heart is prepared, you will come eagerly, joyfully, expectantly. All too often our hearts are not in it. We sing "There Is a Redeemer" (*I wonder how the Chiefs are going to do today?*), "Great Is the LORD" *(It sure is getting hot in here)*, "When We All Get to Heaven" *(I wonder if I should put my money in cryptocurrency?)*.

We come to church busy, hurried, and worried. Maybe we come angry. I am convinced the devil stirs up trouble in Christian families on Sunday morning so he can distract their hearts from worshiping God. Worshiping with a whole heart means we lay aside a critical spirit and join with God's people in praising the Lord. What is the first and greatest commandment? "You shall love the Lord your God with all your heart, all your soul, all your mind and all your strength, then your neighbor as yourself." It is not church work first and then worship. It is worshiping God and loving Him first, and out of that flows everything else.

Lord, help me to worship You with a whole heart today. Amen.

1. How much time did you spend preparing your heart for worship last Sunday?
2. Name the worries and concerns that keep you from focusing on God.
3. Spend a few moments giving those things to the Lord.

WHEN THE FOUNDATIONS ARE DESTROYED

When the foundations are destroyed,
what can the righteous do?

PSALM 11:3

What do you do when life crumbles beneath your feet?

We don't know exactly when David wrote this psalm. Many writers connect it to the time when Saul chased David in the wilderness (1 Sam. 23:13–14), but we can't be sure. We know the psalm comes at a desperate moment when his enemies seem to be closing in on him, and his friends encourage him to run away.

When the foundations are destroyed, there are many things the righteous can do, but above everything else, they must first get a right view of God.

We Will Not Flee

"When you are persecuted in one place, flee to another" (Matt. 10:23).

It is not wrong to flee persecution, but sometimes you can't escape. Sometimes the Lord calls you to stand and face whatever comes. *God's people are not required to prove their faith by staying in one place when they could save their lives by fleeing to the countryside.* After all, David hid from

Saul for years until the time came for him to become king. We have to stand and fight for what we believe. We leave the results in God's hands.

As they say in the Coast Guard, "You have to go out. You don't have to come back."

This is no time to flee, and there is no place to go anyway.

We Will Not Fear

"For look, the wicked bend their bows; they set their arrows against the strings to shoot from the shadows at the upright in heart" (Psalm 11:2).

David is being quite literal. At one point, Saul tried to kill David with a spear. Later he sent his army after him. The arrows they were shooting were not metaphorical. When those arrows hit, they drew blood.

It's always good to know what you are up against. That way you won't be surprised when trouble comes.

We Will Not Fret

"When the foundations are being destroyed, what can the righteous do?" (Psalm 11:3).

The word translated "foundations" refers to the moral and spiritual underpinnings of any society. What can the righteous do when the foundations crumble beneath them? What do you do when the foundations are destroyed? Answer: It all depends on how big your God is. If you've got a small God, you've got a big problem. If you've got a big God, you'll be okay even when the bad guys seem to be winning.

We cannot retreat, and we will not run away. We will not give in to fear. *When the foundations are being destroyed, we need a fresh view of God and a long view of history*. The God who sees all things will judge the wicked and bring them down in the end, and the righteous will see God's face.

When the foundations of society are destroyed, we can say to men and women everywhere, "Christ is the firm foundation, the cornerstone that will never be shaken."

Lord, grant me tenacious, winsome courage as I go through this day. Grant me a cheerful spirit when things don't go my way. Give me the courage to do whatever needs to be done. In Jesus' name, amen.

1. When is it right to run away from danger, and when should we stand and fight?
2. How does our view of God impact our answer to those questions?
3. What does tenacious, winsome courage look like in your life?

HARD TRUTH ABOUT HUMANITY

All have turned aside,
they have together become corrupt;
there is no one who does good, not even one.

PSALM 14:3

Until you know yourself,
you'll never know God.

A mother shocks the world when she straps her two boys into safety seats and then plunges her car into a pond, drowning them. When questioned by the police, she denies any involvement, blaming an unknown assailant. When evidence against her mounts, she finally confesses to murdering her own flesh and blood.

A shudder runs through the national conscience. How could a mother do such a thing? Nothing is more "unnatural" than a mother intentionally harming her children. No explanation will suffice; no excuse can be accepted. This is beyond ordinary right and wrong; we are now in the realm of true moral evil.

A religious leader who makes veiled claims to being the Messiah leads his followers into a standoff with the government. A siege ensues that ends in a fiery conflagration. In a radio interview, one man argues that the leader must have been demon-possessed. Why? Because he did not act like a rational being. The answer must be given that sin by its very nature is not rational.

"There is no one who does good, not even one."

Here is God's evaluation as He looks down from heaven. He doesn't see a single righteous person—not even one. But how can this be? How can God look down at eight billion people and not see even one righteous man? Is this not an overly harsh judgment? The answer is that God judges according to a different standard than the one we use. Most of us grade on the curve.

That is, we look at our neighbor and say, "Well, I'm not as bad as he is." Or we compare ourselves with someone we know at work who makes us look good by comparison.

But God doesn't judge that way. He uses the standard of His own sinless perfection. He compares us to His own perfect holiness, love, wisdom, and justice. And compared with God's own perfection, no one—not even one person—comes close to being righteous in His eyes.

Let us make the matter more personal. There is evil in my heart and in your heart. Evil resides in every human heart. No one is exempt. Some may have a bigger share of evil, some less, but the basic allotment is in there somewhere. If you would know God personally, you must come to grips with who you are.

Take a good look at the man or the woman in the mirror. What you see, you may not like, but you must look anyway. If you don't, you'll never know who you really are. And until you know yourself, you'll never know God, for He never reveals Himself except to people who recognize their need of Him.

Father, show me the truth about myself so that I will cling tightly to Your grace. Amen.

1. Do you agree that there are no "good" people on earth?
2. How then do we explain the millions of unbelievers who apparently live moral lives and who show compassion to others?
3. What standard will God use when He judges your life?

LOVING ALL GOD'S CHILDREN

As for the saints who are in the land, they are the glorious ones in whom is all my delight.

PSALM 16:3

Do you delight in God's children?
Do other Christians seem glorious to you? Hmmm.

In this verse, David uses a word that means "excellent" or "noble" or "gallant" to describe those who know the Lord. That's an unusual way to put it. Perhaps you've heard this little couplet: *To live up above with the saints that we love, that will be glory. But to live down below with the saints that we know, that's another story.*

We chuckle because it's true. But consider this: Do you love all the saints or only some of them? Or do you prefer the saints who think and act like you, who treat you well and hang out with you and see the world the way you do?

We love all the saints some of the time. And we love some of the saints all the time, but some of them are hard to love. Some of them act snotty toward us. Some of them have weird beliefs. We're not even sure some of the "saints" are really saints. We find it easier to love people who believe just like us. We love PLU—People Like Us.

It's quite a challenge if you think about loving all of God's people everywhere, all the time. It requires an adjustment of our thinking, a broadening of our horizons, an opening of our eyes, a willingness to love those with whom we disagree, and it even means we'll love some unlovely people.

The biblical concept of brotherly love comes from a word meaning "tender affection owed to those born from the same womb." It's easy to understand why the early Christians adopted this word to describe Christian love. All Christians have been "born of the same womb" through the new birth. To be born again means to receive new life through personal faith in Jesus Christ.

I have three brothers—Andy, Alan, and Ron. I am the second of four Pritchard brothers. We live in four different states—Kansas, Alabama, Tennessee, and Arkansas. We have different personalities, different habits and hobbies, different likes and dislikes. Yet we come from the same womb. That fact means there is a special place in my heart for my brothers. Even if I haven't seen them for a long time, it's as if I last saw them yesterday. There is a bond between us that time and distance cannot break.

The same truth applies in the spiritual realm. Everyone who belongs to Jesus belongs to me, and I owe them tender affection and brotherly love. Take a good look at your fellow believers. They are precious, gallant, noble, and glorious. That's how God sees them.

When the love of God captures us, our hearts will be as big as His—reaching the ends of the earth.

Lord God, teach me to love as You love—with a heart as big as Yours—and with arms that reach out to embrace all Your children. Amen.

1. Why is unity essential in the local church?
2. What happens when a church loses its unity?
3. Think of a step you could take today to reach out to a Christian brother or sister who comes from a different background.

DEATH IS NOT THE END OF OUR STORY

Therefore my heart is glad and
my tongue rejoices; my body also
will rest secure, because you will not
abandon me to the grave, nor will
you let your Holy One see decay.

PSALM 16:9–10

You're going to die someday.
That's a fact. What happens then?

We all face that question sooner or later. When David thought about it, these verses were his answer. He knew God would not abandon him in the hour of his greatest need.

What happens to believers the moment they die? Here is God's answer: Those who have trusted Jesus Christ as Savior go immediately into the presence of the Lord. They are "away from the body" and "at home with the Lord" (2 Cor. 5:8). As the apostle Paul languishes in a Roman jail, he expresses a desire to depart from his earthly body and its troubles and to be with Christ in heaven. In his mind, dying would be "gain" because it would usher him into the personal presence of Jesus Christ (Phil. 1:21–23). Jesus made the same promise to the thief on the cross: "Today you will be with Me in paradise" (Luke 23:43).

Meanwhile, the body is buried, awaiting the day of resurrection. That's what David meant when he declared God would not abandon him to the grave forever. Peter applied this verse to Christ's resurrection in Acts 2:31–32. Since our resurrection is linked with Christ's, these words of David apply directly to us. Because Christ arose, we too shall someday rise from the dead.

Ponder the implications of this truth. All believers in Christ will be raised. That includes people who died two thousand years ago, like James and John and Peter, and believers who died fifteen hundred years ago, five hundred years ago, one hundred years ago, fifty years ago, ten years ago, one year ago, one month ago, and those who died in Christ this week. It includes Martin Luther, John Calvin, Peter Lombard, Charles Spurgeon, D. L. Moody, Billy Sunday, and Jim Elliot.

It will be a literal resurrection from the dead. This includes the resurrection of those who die at sea, those whose bodies are cremated, those who die on the battlefield, and those who die a lingering death from cancer. They will be raised indestructible with brand-new bodies, clothed with immortality, healed, restored, put in their right minds, raised to live forever, raised to die no more.

I ran across a beautiful phrase from the Pulpit Commentary that lifts my heart every time I read it. There will be "victory on the last battlefield." Life is a series of battles for all of us, and we all "take it on the chin" sooner or later. But in the last battle—the struggle with death—there is victory for the children of God.

Let the people of God rejoice. Death is not the end of our story.

Rock of Ages, place before my eyes the glorious prospect of future resurrection and fill me with such heavenly longing that the world can have no hold on me. Amen.

1. Do you believe in the resurrection of the dead?
2. Why is this doctrine essential to the Christian faith?
3. Think of at least five names you could add to the list of believers now dead who will be raised when Christ returns.

WHY ARE YOU HERE?

You have made known to me the path of life;
you will fill me with joy in your presence,
with eternal pleasures at your right hand.

PSALM 16:11

Do you know why God put you where you are right now?

That's a tough question for some of us to answer.

Have you wondered about that? Why has God put you where you are right now? Does it happen by chance that you are single (or married), with children at home (or long since moved away), with a good job (or stuck in a bad situation)? Or is there a larger purpose at work in your life?

Let me ask that question from a completely different perspective: What will you have to show for your life when you stand before Jesus Christ? A good job? A college degree? Money in the bank? Lots of friends? A large reputation? A successful career? The praise of others?

If that's all you've got to show for your life, then you really don't have much going for you. Sooner than you think, you'll be lying in a box six feet underground with grass growing over your head, and all the things of this life won't matter at all. Someone else will have your money and your job. Your fame will fade, your glory will disappear, and everything you now own will belong to others. You will eventually be forgotten except by those people who stumble on your gravestone a hundred years from now and say, "I wonder who this guy was."

Howard Hendricks said it this way: "Only two things in this world are eternal—the Word of God and people. It only makes sense to build your life around those things that will last forever." The Word of God will last forever. People last forever. Everything else disappears.

When asked by a job interviewer about his goal in life, one man responded: "My goal in life is to go to heaven and to take as many people with me as possible." That's a thoroughly biblical worldview.

Some years ago, I heard Dr. Vernon Grounds say that whenever we are faced with a major decision, we ought to ask ourselves, "What difference will this make in ten thousand years?" Most of the things we worry so much about won't matter in three weeks, let alone three months or three years. We focus on the trivial and forget to pursue the eternal. But ten thousand times ten thousand years from now, you'll still be glad you invested your life for Jesus Christ.

Lord of all things, help me to invest now in those things that will pay eternal dividends. Amen.

1. Go back through this entry and answer each question.
2. Why do you think God put you where you are right now?
3. As you think about the things you have done in the last week, which ones won't matter in ten thousand years?

HOW A SLAVE TRADER MET JESUS

He reached down from on high and took hold of me; he drew me out of deep waters.

PSALM 18:16

Did you know that the author of the hymn "Amazing Grace" was a former slave trader?

That's part of our story for today. But first, just a word about Psalm 18. David wrote this exuberant praise song after the Lord delivered him from the hand of Saul. Saul had become so enraged he lost his mind. For months he tracked down David in the desert and tried to kill him. But each time the Lord delivered him from Saul's murderous schemes.

When it was over, David wrote this psalm of praise so the world would know what God had done for him. God had "reached down from on high" and drew him out of "deep waters."

Have you ever felt like that?

That's John Newton's story. He was born in 1725, the son of an English sea captain. At the age of eleven, he went to sea for the first time. Forced to join the Royal Navy, he tried to escape but was arrested in West Africa. He became the slave of a white slave trader's black wife. For two years, he lived in hunger and destitution.

He eventually became a slave ship captain, taking black Africans to the Mediterranean and the West Indies. In 1747, he boarded a ship for England, but a violent storm in the North Atlantic hit the boat, which began to fill with water. The timbers broke away from the side. An ordinary boat would have gone to the bottom immediately, but they were carrying a load of beeswax and wool that was lighter than water.

During the struggle to save the ship, the young man said to himself almost without thinking, "If this will not do, the Lord have mercy on us." By his own words, it was the first desire for mercy he had felt in many years. That was the turning point of his life.

He left the slave trade and later entered the ministry in Olney, England. He soon became known as a great preacher who attracted enormous crowds. He wrote nearly three hundred hymns—most of which have long since been forgotten. But he wrote one song that is perhaps the most famous hymn ever. Around the world, Christians sing it in dozens of languages:

Amazing grace! how sweet the sound
That saved a wretch like me!
I once was lost, but now am found,
Was blind, but now I see.

Before he died, he prepared his own epitaph, which reads: "John Newton, once an infidel and libertine, a servant of slaves in Africa, was, by the rich mercy of our Lord and Savior Jesus Christ, preserved, restored, pardoned, and appointed to preach the faith he had long labored to destroy."

That's what God can do. That's true conversion.

Holy Father, when I was drowning in the deep water of sin, You pulled me to safety. Use me, Lord, to do the same for others who need to know Jesus! Amen.

1. What is your testimony of God's grace in your life?
2. Take a moment and rehearse your own story.
3. Now pray that God will give you a chance to tell someone this week.

A LESSON FROM THE OBSERVATORY

The heavens declare the glory of God; the skies proclaim the work of his hands.

PSALM 19:1

Not many churches have an observatory.

I know of exactly one church with an observatory, and I know it because I pastored that church for seventeen years. The church owned a building that had been built by the Presbyterians a hundred years earlier.

They included an observatory on top of the educational building when they built it. In my day, the only way to get there was by clambering up a winding metal staircase (in the dark) that led to a cramped room perched on the roof.

It had obviously not been used in many years, but it had the familiar vaulted ceiling with an opening for a telescope. The stand was still there, but the telescope was long gone.

In that musty, dusty, cramped space, I could imagine generations of young boys and girls looking up into the stars, searching for Venus and Jupiter and Saturn, and searching for the Big Dipper and Leo and Aquarius.

As I peered into the gloom of that cramped space, I saw this emblazoned on the ceiling, "The heavens declare the glory of God" (Ps. 19:1). The builders of that church understood what David meant when he wrote those words. The sky itself testifies to God's glory.

- The galaxies shout, "He is here!"
- The stars sing together, "The Lord made the heavens."
- The comets all declare, "The Creator reigns over His creation."

According to David, the heavens speak in a language all can hear. The stars sing, and the planets preach. The far-off galaxies declare God's glory. Perhaps that's why the astronauts on Apollo 8 read Genesis 1 to a worldwide audience as they orbited the moon on Christmas Eve, 1968. Three men in a tiny capsule hurtling through space reminded everyone that "in the beginning God created the heavens and the earth" (Gen. 1:1).

No one can miss the message.

In 1901 Maltbie Babcock penned these enduring words:

This is my Father's world,
And to my list'ning ears
All nature sings, and round me rings
The music of the spheres.
This is my Father's world:
I rest me in the thought
Of rocks and trees, of skies and seas—
his hand the wonders wrought.

God has left His fingerprints everywhere. He signed His name to everything He made. The earth is marked "Made by God" in letters so big that no one fails to see it.

Go outside tonight and count the twinkling stars. Each one declares the glory of God!

Creator of the universe, give me eyes to see
Your handiwork, ears to hear Your voice,
and lips to proclaim Your greatness. Amen.

1. How does the vast night sky show us God's handiwork?
2. What can people learn about God by looking at His universe?
3. Why would a church build an observatory?

READ THE BIBLE LIKE YOU EAT CANDY

The ordinances of the LORD ... are sweeter than honey from the honeycomb.

PSALM 19:9–10

In the ancient world, honey was the universal sweetener.

Back then, people used honey the way we use sugar and artificial sweeteners. *The writer is telling us he has a "sweet tooth" for God's Word.* That is an unusual and perhaps even a strange thought to most of us.

To us sweetness speaks of chocolate cake and fresh donuts. We don't normally think of sweetness when we read the Bible. After all, this is a big book filled with history and doctrine and prophecy and lots of words that are hard to pronounce. Plus, the Bible is printed in a big book that is often quite bulky. It's hard to associate the thought of sweetness with the Bible.

Think of a piece of hard candy. How do you eat it? You put it in your mouth and let it dissolve slowly. As it dissolves, the sweetness fills your mouth. If you try to put 20 pieces of candy in your mouth, they won't fit, and you'll spit them out. The sweetness you seek comes slowly, one piece at a time. Martin Luther said the way to study the Bible is to pick a verse and shake it like a fruit tree. If you keep shaking a verse, the fruit will fall in your lap sooner or later. Luther also said if the fruit doesn't fall, go to another verse. Eventually you will find a verse where the fruit falls in abundance. There you can stop and feast on God's Word.

Consider the familiar words of Psalm 23:1, "The Lord is my shepherd; I shall not want" (KJV). Roll that around in your mind for a moment. It is the Lord Himself who shepherds me. And He is my shepherd at all times, in every situation, no matter where I am or what I am doing. Even when I stray from Him, He never leaves my side. And even though He is the shepherd for others, He is a personal shepherd—*my shepherd*—known by me, and I am known to Him. Therefore, I do not want; I will not want; I cannot lack for any good thing. I have never been in want, I am not in want now (no matter my circumstances), and I will not be in want tomorrow. Such a shepherd is my Lord to me.

Now that's very simple, isn't it? And much more could be added. But even as I wrote those words, I felt the fruit falling all around me. *This is how the Word of God becomes sweet to us*—word by word, phrase by phrase, verse by verse. If we savor it, its sweetness will fill our hearts.

Lord, implant in me a love for Your Word. May the fruit of Your Word fill my heart today. Amen.

1. Take a look at Philippians 2:14–15 and think about each word.
2. What is God saying to you from these two verses?
3. How can you savor these truths in the same way that you savor a candy?

AN EVERYDAY PRAYER

May the words of my mouth
and the meditation of my heart be
pleasing in your sight, O Lord,
my Rock and my Redeemer.

PSALM 19:14

If you want a simple prayer, here it is.

The closing verse of Psalm 19 teaches us what we already know—that we need God's help so that our words and thoughts might please Him. In the preceding two verses, David cried out to God for cleansing from "hidden faults" and "willful sins."

Sometimes we sin and don't even know it; other times we sin openly. Both cases desperately need God's forgiveness so that we might be "blameless" in His eyes (v. 13).

It is not wrong to receive praise from men, especially for a job well done. Good work ought to be praised. However, it's wrong to do your work solely—or even mostly—to receive the praise of man. We don't need spiritual groupies or some kind of spiritual PR department to make us feel better about ourselves. What we want and seek is the praise of almighty God.

If we seek the praise of others, we will have it—and that is all we will have. Pleasing God is something else entirely. Let's compare those two ideas for just a moment.

People Pleaser:

- Refuses to speak hard truth.
- Often speaks too quickly.
- Makes excuses when confronted.
- Makes too many promises.
- Obedient when convenient.
- Unwilling to offend over issues of truth.

God Pleaser:

- Seeks God first.
- Ready to admit when wrong.
- Not hasty to speak.
- Nothing hidden because there is nothing to hide.
- Speaks the truth in love.
- Willing to offend in order to be faithful to God.

Let us suppose you have been feeling sick lately. When you go to the doctor, he administers a test. The results are not good. The outlook is grim, but the disease is treatable if you get started now. What do you want the doctor to do? If he tells you the truth, you'll be devastated. If he doesn't, you'll be dead. Would you rather have him sugarcoat the truth or even lie to you? Or do you want to know the whole truth about your condition?

I know the answer for me. When I go to the doctor, I want to know the whole truth, even if it hurts. But what if he says, "I want to spare you pain"? "Doc, tell that to my wife and children at my funeral," I reply.

When life-and-death issues are at stake, only the truth will do. When it comes to the gospel of Jesus Christ, the stakes couldn't be higher. Christians must hold to the highest possible standards of truth and integrity. There is no other way to please God.

Lord Jesus, raise me above the smiles and frowns of this world so that my only concern will be Your approval. Amen.

1. Are you a people-pleaser or a God-pleaser?
2. What would your friends say about you?
3. Why is truth-telling an essential part of pleasing God?

THE FORSAKEN CHRIST

My God, my God,
why have you forsaken me?
PSALM 22:1

The end is near. That much is clear.

Jesus is at the point of death. Whatever happened in those three hours of darkness has brought Him to death's door. His strength is nearly gone, the struggle almost over. His chest heaves with every breath, His moans now are only whispers.

Instinctively the crowd pushes closely to watch His last moments. From those parched lips comes a cry drawn from Psalm 22: "My God, my God, why have you forsaken me?"

What does it mean?

Imagine that somewhere in the universe there is a cesspool containing all the sins that have ever been committed. The cesspool is deep, dark, and indescribably foul. Now imagine that while Jesus was on the cross, that cesspool was emptied onto Him. See the flow of filth as it settles upon Him. The flow never seems to stop. It is vile, toxic, deadly, and filled with disease, pain, and suffering.

When God looked down at His Son, He saw the cesspool of sin emptied on His head. No wonder He turned away from the sight. Who could bear to watch it?

Think of it. All the lust in the world was there. All the

broken promises were there. All the murder, all the killing, all the hatred between people. Every vile deed and wicked thought, every vain imagination—all of it was laid upon Jesus when He hung on the cross.

I take from this solemn truth two significant implications:

First, we must never minimize the horror of human sin. It was our sin that Jesus bore that day. Our sin caused the Father to turn away from the Son. It was our sin floating in that cesspool of iniquity. He became a curse, and we were part of the reason. Let us never joke about sin. It is no laughing matter.

Second, we must never minimize the awful cost of our salvation. Without the Cross there would be no forgiveness and no salvation. Without the Cross we would be lost forever. It cost Christ everything to redeem us. Let us never make light of what cost Him so dearly.

This cry from the Cross is for all the lonely people of the world. It is for the abandoned child—the widow—the divorcee struggling to make ends meet—the mother standing over the bed of her suffering daughter—the father out of work—the parents left alone—the prisoner in his cell—the aged persons who languish in convalescent homes—wives abandoned by their husbands—singles who celebrate their birthdays alone.

This is the word from the Cross for you. No one has ever been as alone as Jesus was. You will never be forsaken as He was. No cry of your pain can exceed the cry of His pain when God turned His back and looked the other way.

Lord Jesus, You bore the weight of my sins that I might bear them no more. You were forsaken that I might never be alone. I cannot repay You, but I will praise You forever for so great a salvation. Amen.

1. How could God the Father "forsake" His Son at the Cross?
2. What does that tell you about the cost of your salvation?
3. Take a few moments to contemplate the Cross, and to praise God that the price for sin has been fully paid.

THE VERDICT OVERTURNED

All who see me mock me;
they hurl insults, shaking their heads:
"He trusts in the Lord*; let the* Lord *rescue him."*

PSALM 22:7–8

This is what they said about Jesus.
You can read about it in Matthew 27:43.

When Jesus walked on the face of the earth, many people thought He was a criminal. The Pharisees, Sadducees, and the temple aristocrats thought He was a criminal. They considered Him a rabble-rouser. Some of them even said He was filled with demons.

Do you remember that? Jesus was working miracles, and they said, *He does it by the power of the devil* (see Matt. 12:22–24). That's really the whole story of His ministry.

The common people believed in Him, but the power brokers concluded that Jesus was not a righteous man:

- "He's not a good man. He's a bad man."
- "He's not a force for good. He's a force for evil."
- "He didn't come from heaven. He really came from hell."
- "He's not doing the work of God. He's really doing the work of Satan."
- "He never had the power of God. He's really filled with demons."

They decided He was a kind of religious mad dog who had to be eliminated for the public good. Ultimately, they said, "We've got to get rid of Him." So, they executed Him as a criminal. And it appeared when they had executed Him that they were right. On Friday afternoon it seemed like He was nothing but a ne'er-do-well, just another in that long series of Galilean traveling prophets, just another con artist, just another charismatic rabbi who stirs up the public and then comes to no good end.

They appeared to be right for about thirty-six hours. They woke up Saturday morning, and they were right. They ate lunch Saturday, and they were right. They went to bed Saturday night, and they were right.

But when they woke up Sunday morning, they were wrong. Something unexpected happened between sundown Saturday night and sunrise Sunday morning.

In our political process, you can appeal the case upward if you're found guilty at a lower level. Finally, you will come to the Supreme Court—the court of last resort. If the case makes it to the Supreme Court, the justices can overturn any guilty verdict.

On Sunday morning, earth's verdict was overturned, and heaven spoke in favor of the Son of God. A mighty hand reached down and rolled away the stone, and the Son of God walked out from the realm of death, never to die again. When He rose from the dead, that was God's way of saying, "Not Guilty. This Man is My Son. Hear Him."

Father, thank You for proving once and for all that Jesus really is Your only begotten Son. Amen.

1. If Jesus was God's Son, why didn't everyone recognize that fact?
2. Why do many people today still doubt His true identity?
3. How did the Resurrection overturn the world's verdict?

OUR GOOD SHEPHERD

The Lord is my shepherd,
I shall not be in want.

PSALM 23:1

Israel has always been a nation of shepherds.

To this day, shepherds herd their flocks in the hills around Bethlehem. Abraham was a shepherd, and so was David, who wrote the words of this beloved psalm. We are told in 1 Samuel 16 that while David was tending sheep for his father Jesse, he was chosen to be the king of Israel. Psalm 78:71 tells us that "from tending the sheep [the Lord] brought [David] to be the shepherd of His people Jacob."

David was a shepherd in some sense throughout his entire life, so it is not surprising that he considered the Lord his shepherd.

It is sometimes alleged that sheep are dumb, but that is not true. Sheep are smart animals who tend to lose their way without a shepherd to lead them. They go astray from the flock (Isa. 53:6), they fall prey to vicious animals, they cannot find their way to the fold, and if someone does not come and rescue them (Luke 15:3–7), they will die in the wilderness.

Sheep need a shepherd who cares for them. A good shepherd is everything to the sheep. He lives with them twenty-four hours a day, eats with them, sleeps with them, and leads them from pasture to quiet waters, constantly watching lest his flock be overtaken by savage wolves.

The shepherd is a guide, a helper, a friend, a protector, a leader, a provider, and a healer for the wounded. What a shepherd is for the sheep, the Lord Jesus is for His people. "I am the good shepherd. The good shepherd lays down His life for the sheep" (John 10:11). We need to ponder these words because we live in a world where trust in leaders is at an all-time low. There was a time when public officials, business leaders, doctors, teachers, and clergy were universally trusted.

If you had a title, possessed a degree, or held public office, people assumed they could trust you. Our generation has witnessed a series of shocking revelations from the White House to the courthouse to the church house that, taken together, have eroded public confidence. We live in a poisoned atmosphere where anyone in a position of authority is subject to intense scrutiny.

Yet amid our doubt, we still need leaders we can trust. When Jesus lists His qualifications, He simply says, "I am the good shepherd." He proved it by laying down His life for us.

Here is good news for a cynical generation. If you're looking for someone to trust, take a long look at Jesus. He's the Shepherd we need.

Loving Shepherd, help me to love You,
follow You, and trust You more
today than yesterday. Amen.

1. Name five qualities of a good shepherd. How does the Lord Jesus fulfill each one?
2. Why is trust such a vital quality?
3. What happens when leaders lose the trust of their followers?

THE SHADOW OF DEATH

Even though I walk through
the valley of the shadow of death,
I will fear no evil, for you are with me.
PSALM 23:4

How can we walk beside
someone who is walking through
the valley of the shadow of death?

I went to see someone who was dying of cancer. When I arrived, she was clearly down to her last few days. I held her hand and recited the great promises of God about heaven. Someone in the room said she was afraid to die. I told her I wasn't an expert on death, but I know someone who is. I told her I know someone who had died and come back from the dead. His name is Jesus. He holds the keys of death and Hades in His hands.

I held her hand and said, "When the moment comes, don't be afraid. Just call out the name Jesus, and He will come for you." I told her that I don't know about death by personal experience, but I know who stands at the door to make sure we make it safely through to the other side. Then I quoted some verses from Psalm 23, "Yea, though I walk through the valley of the shadow of death, I will fear no evil: for thou art with me. Thy rod and thy staff, they comfort me. … Surely goodness and mercy shall follow me all the days of my life and I shall dwell in the house of the Lord forever" (KJV).

Then I prayed, and someone in the room started to sing, "What a friend we have in Jesus." We all started to sing, and I heard her singing with us. Even at death's door, she was holding on to Jesus.

Brothers and sisters, we're going to make it! God has willed it so. We will all eventually go through the valley of the shadow of death. We need a guide who can help us on that treacherous journey. We need someone who's been there before.

Who can we get? Where can we find a guide like that? His name is Jesus! He's been there before. He knows the way through. He's been to the light on the other side, and He'll come for us.

Thank God, we don't walk through that valley alone. Jesus will walk with us. He'll lead us through to the other side.

The saints of God have nothing to fear in the moment of death. Though it may not be pleasant or painless, though it comes after long-suffering or in a fiery crash, the moment itself will be filled with joy as the Lord Himself escorts God's children through the darkest valley of all. At that moment, all other guides must turn back. Only the Lord Jesus Christ can help us through.

Cheer up, child of God. Smile through your tears. Death is the worst that can happen to us. The best is yet to come.

Almighty God, thank You that death cannot cancel Your promises to Your children. We will not fear as long as You are walking next to us. Amen.

1. Is there a difference between being afraid of death and being afraid to die?
2. How does knowing Jesus give us courage when life on earth ends?
3. What will happen when you die?

GOOD NEWS FOR WAYWARD SHEEP

He makes me lie down in
green pastures, he leads
me beside quiet waters,
he restores my soul.

PSALM 23:2–3

If the Lord is your Shepherd,
you have everything you need.

Matthew Henry commented that Christians everywhere have sung Psalm 23, "and will be while the world stands, with a great deal of pleasure and satisfaction." Those words still ring true three hundred years later. The twenty-third Psalm may well be the most familiar passage in the Bible. Our children learn it by heart almost from the time they know how to read. It is the psalm for every season of life.

"Shepherd" may seem a homely name for God, yet it reveals an essential part of His character. All that a shepherd does to protect and provide for his sheep, the Lord does for His children. The present tense of the first verse is crucial. The Lord is my Shepherd—not just that He was or will be in the distant future. Friends come and go, even beloved family members die, but the eternal God is our eternal Shepherd—today, tomorrow, and forever.

Verse 2 contains three lovely pictures of a shepherd's care of his sheep: First, he provides rest: "He makes me lie down in green pastures." The flock needs a safe place to rest, and the shepherd must find it, because the sheep can't do it on their own. So, the shepherd searches out a lush meadow filled with green grass, not arid desert or rocky soil. There the hungry sheep feed, and there they rest before moving on.

Second, there is refreshment: "He leads me beside quiet waters." Literally, "waters of resting places," speaking of an oasis in the desert. The shepherd knows where the water is, and he leads the sheep to water because they would never find it on their own.

Third, there is restoration: "He restores my soul." The word *restore* has within it the idea of returning a thing to its original condition. Here, it means the Lord will provide everything I need so that my soul will no longer hunger and thirst. As a good meal at the end of a hard day restores the body, so the Lord "restores" the soul of those who trust in Him. If it is true that "we all, like sheep, have gone astray" (Isa. 53:6), it is also true that the Lord Himself restores us.

The Shepherd comes to where we have fallen, bends over us, encourages us, picks us up, and carries us safely home again. And He does it every time we lose our way. It is because the Lord restores my soul again and again that I will dwell in the house of the Lord forever.

God promises to do all this for those who follow Him. Right now we're on a journey, a pilgrimage from earth to heaven. We're on our way home. The road often seems long and lonely.

Fear not, child of God. If the Lord is your Shepherd, you have everything you need—now and forever.

Father, You have provided
all I need and more besides.
Thank You for an overabundance of grace,
because I'm going to need all of it today. Amen.

1. Have you ever memorized Psalm 23? If not, take a few moments to read it aloud several times.
2. Write out Psalm 23 phrase by phrase, adding your own personal application words.
3. How has the Lord "restored" your soul recently?

JUST SAY NO

Who may ascend the hill of the Lord?
Who may stand in his holy place? He who has
clean hands and a pure heart, who does not
lift up his soul to an idol or swear by what is false.
PSALM 24:3–4

These verses tell us not everyone
is welcome in God's presence.

God welcomes those with clean hands and pure hearts. Those who have chosen a sinful lifestyle should think twice before coming glibly before the Lord. Dirty hands are not welcome in "His holy place."

When God says, "Be holy because I, the Lord your God, am holy" (Lev. 19:2), it means: "Be pure for I am pure," and "Be clean for I am clean," and especially "Be different for I am different."

Strange as it may seem, practical holiness begins with the negative. That is to say, holiness is more than what you do. It's also what you don't do.

- It's more than where you go; it's also where you won't go.
- It's more than what you say; it's also what you won't say.
- It's more than what you watch on TV; it's also what you won't watch.
- It's more than the websites you visit on the internet;

it's also the website you won't visit.

- It's more than what you wear; it's also what you won't wear.
- It's more than what you worship; it's also what you won't worship.
- It's more than who your friends are, it's also who your friends aren't.
- It's more than who you sleep with; it's also who you don't sleep with.

Why should there be a negative emphasis? I can think of at least two answers.

1. When the world looks at us, the easiest difference to see is in the negative.
2. Until we are set apart from sin, we are not yet ready to be separated to God and His service.

Suppose I ask my wife out for a special date, and I tell her we're going someplace nice. The appointed hour comes, and I show up in dirty overalls, I stink, my hair is filthy, my hands are greasy, and my nose is running. Meanwhile, my wife is dressed in her prettiest outfit waiting for me. Now, will she go out with me? Yes or no? No, because I haven't shown proper respect for her. Does she still love me? Yes. But she's not going out with me like that. I can go, but I'll be going alone if I do. I'm not ready to go out with her until I get cleaned up.

In the very same way, as long as my life is unclean, I'm not ready to go anywhere with God. I haven't shown Him proper respect and honor.

Does He still love me? Yes. But until my life is clean, I'll be going by myself.

My Lord, make me holy as You are holy.
You alone can answer this prayer. Amen.

1. Why does practical holiness begin with the negative?
2. What happens when we neglect God's call to moral purity in the "small areas" of life?
3. Pray for clean hands and a pure heart so that you can come before the Lord with a clear conscience.

CHOOSE YOUR FRIENDS WISELY

I do not sit with deceitful men,
nor do I consort with hypocrites.

PSALM 26:4

Not every acquaintance should become a friend, and not every friend should become a close friend. Choose wisely.

The email message told a sad but not unfamiliar story:

> Years ago, I accepted Christ into my heart. At first, I wanted to do His will and live a Christian life. I have slipped quite a bit since then. I wanted to experience all that I was told not to do, and I did. I thought I was happy, but inside I was crying out for help.
>
> I latched onto a group of friends that weren't exactly following the right path. The friendship quickly died. Then I joined another group of friends that had an even worse effect on my life. I thought they were true friends and again Christ disagreed (I didn't realize it till now though). I was stuck pretty much friendless this year, living on my own. I couldn't understand what was wrong with my personality and why it was so hard to keep friends. I now understand that God had a plan

> to destroy those dangerous relationships.
>
> I asked God to take me back tonight and have not stopped crying since. I guess I am asking you to pray for me because I don't want to lose this desire. I want to change and do God's will. I know true happiness comes from seeing Jesus and I want a clear picture. It is so hard to be alone, but if I put Christ first, He will be all I need.

As I reflect on this letter, it occurs to me it might have been written by many people I know. Change a detail here or there, and it might be one of a hundred personal stories. It speaks to the awesome power of relationships for good or for evil.

No relationship stays static. *Relationships are like rivers that continually flow this way or that.* Every friendship either pulls us up toward God or drags us down toward hell.

Some people don't belong in your life. It's okay to let them go. Some people drag us down. It's okay to move on from them. You're on a journey with the Lord. If some people don't want to travel with you, that's on them, not you. Let them go and keep walking with Jesus.

Not every acquaintance should become a friend, and not every friend should become a close friend. Choose wisely. We become like the friends we choose.

Lord Jesus, I pray for the discernment to choose friends who will bring me closer to You. Amen.

1. Think about your five closest friends. What spiritual impact have they had on your life?
2. What impact have you had on them?
3. Do you need to make some changes in this area?

EASTER, ABRAHAM, AND UNANSWERED PRAYER

My heart says of you, "Seek his face!"
Your face, Lord, I will seek. Do not hide
your face from me, do not turn your servant
away in anger; you have been my helper.

PSALM 27:8–9

Why are some prayers not answered?

Surely one of the biggest frustrations of the Christian life is the mystery of unanswered prayer. Who among us has not prayed and prayed for something only to have the heavens turn to brass? And who among us has not eventually stopped praying because the answer never came? Why isn't every prayer answered immediately?

We come to God as children, with a child's limited perspective, with sometimes childish attitudes, and with a child's expectation of immediate response. The answer is not to stop praying, but to keep praying. And the father who knows us better than we know ourselves will sometimes say "Yes," sometimes will say "No," and sometimes will say "Let's wait a while on that one."

Genesis 18 tells the story of Abraham asking God to spare Sodom if enough righteous men can be found within it. Sodom and Gomorrah were so exceedingly wicked that

God determined to destroy them by fire. Abraham knew what God intended to do and began to pray for Sodom. He knew Lot was there, and he presumed other righteous men were there, so he said to the Lord, "Will you destroy the righteous along with the wicked?" Then Abraham began to bargain with God. Would you spare it if there are 50 righteous men? Then 45. Then 40. Then 30. Then 20. Then 10.

God agreed to spare the city if ten righteous men could be found. In one sense, Abraham's faith is getting weaker and stronger at the same time. He doesn't have much faith in the men of Sodom; righteous men were scarce. But as he prays, his faith in the mercy and justice of God is growing. He understands more about God than he did before.

Did God answer Abraham's prayer? Yes, but not in the way he expected. Sodom and Gomorrah were destroyed by fire and brimstone. But in praying the way he did, Abraham learned that prayer is more than simply asking for what we want. *The prayer that changes the world first changes us.*

What Abraham asked for did not happen, but Lot (a righteous man who had compromised far too much) was delivered along with his daughters. But his wife turned into a pillar of salt. In the end, Abraham learned God's wisdom was far higher than his own. That is a lesson we all must learn again and again.

Each year when we celebrate Easter, we are reminded that God's ways are not our ways. The disciples were not expecting a resurrection, yet God answered with an empty tomb. We may rest assured that when we do our part, God will not fail to do His. For the Christian, every day is Easter and every prayer an opportunity for God to surprise us with an unexpected answer.

All-knowing Father, I trust in You even when I do not understand. Thank You for loving me enough to sometimes say "no" to my prayers. Amen.

1. Looking back, can you think of some prayers you are glad God didn't answer?
2. How can unanswered prayer be a benefit to us?
3. How can we keep our faith strong even while our prayers remain unanswered?

BIBLICAL OPTIMISM

I am still confident of this: I will see the goodness of the LORD *in the land of the living.*

PSALM 27:13

Are you an optimist or a pessimist?

For most of us, the answer to the question above is: *It depends*. By that we mean it depends on our circumstances. But biblical optimism is based on God's promises and not your circumstances.

That's a crucial principle to grasp. You may be facing difficult circumstances right now, and your tendency might be to think, *Psalm 27:13 doesn't apply to me.* You may be going through a tough time financially, and you think nothing could ever change this. Or your marriage may be in trouble and divorce may seem the only option. You may be on the verge of losing your job. Or your health. Or a dream you've pursued for many years. There may be trouble in your family or at school or on the job. And as you survey the situation, you can't find any grounds for encouragement.

That doesn't matter. It is still possible to be optimistic because biblical optimism rests on the promises of the gospel and not on your circumstances. As long as the gospel is true (and it is), significant change is possible, even in apparently hopeless situations.

That perspective changes the way we look at disappointment and discouragement. If God's number one goal is to make me like Jesus Christ (see Rom. 8:28–29), then He has many lessons to teach me. Most of those lessons can only come through heartache and difficulty because we learn more through the hard times than through the good times.

God's work in your life is chipping away at your weak points and slowly developing the character of Jesus Christ within. But that means there are tremendous grounds for optimism—even in the worst situations—because the hard times mean God is hard at work in you to make you more like His Son.

Nothing is wasted. Nothing that happens to you is meant to destroy you. Even the attacks and slanders of your enemies are allowed by God for a higher purpose in your life. Everything has a purpose in your life. Everything. The fact you don't always see it doesn't negate that fact. So be encouraged. God is at work in your life, especially in the hard times.

Lord of my life, give me long-range vision to see that even my difficulties have a purpose in Your eternal plan. Amen.

1. Are you a biblical optimist?
2. Name three places you have seen "the goodness of the Lord" in your own life in the last week.
3. Name several areas of your life that are still "under construction" by God.

TAKING THE LONG VIEW OF LIFE

For his anger lasts only a moment, but his favor lasts a lifetime; weeping may remain for a night, but rejoicing comes in the morning.

PSALM 30:5

There are no shortcuts to spiritual maturity.

The following message came from a young man in a state penitentiary:

> Prison has been a place to grow spiritually. Everything Satan does against me God can and will use to his glory. "And we know that all things work together for good to them that love God, to them who are the called according to his purpose" (Romans 8:28 KJV).
>
> A few days ago, I got a letter from the Parole Board. They put off my parole for at least two more years. Please don't feel sorry for me. Rejoice with me. Remember God created the earth in six days. Just imagine what He can do in my life in two more years.

I'm going to take his advice and not feel sorry for him. As bad as it is to be in prison, it's good to be there if it brings you back to God. And it's better to be in prison in the will of God than to be on the streets and far from Him. There are many kinds of freedom in the world and many kinds of bondage. Though my friend is not a free man legally, he is freer today than many people I know.

After I told this story to my congregation, a young, well-dressed man came up to speak with me. Speaking with deep emotion, he said, "Pastor, you don't know this, but I've spent time in prison. I've been exactly where that man is today. And what you said is true. It doesn't matter what got you there; it only matters how you respond."

Although I wish it were not so, many people who read these words are going through hard times right now. As I thought about the matter, I concluded that even if I had the power (which I don't have), I wouldn't take the pain away or make the hard times disappear. God has ordained that your trials are part of His plan to make you like Jesus.

Were I to take away the pain, I might move too soon and block God's work in your life. Because I see things from a human perspective, I might actually hurt you instead of helping you, even though my motives would be good.

It is not "good" to suffer, but suffering is good if it leads us back to the Lord. The Bible tells us that weeping may endure for a night, but joy comes in the morning.

Let us, therefore, endure our trials with grace and even with joy, knowing that in the end, the clouds will part, and the sun will shine again.

When I feel like giving up on life,
Lord, grant me the gift of endurance
so I won't give up on You. Amen.

1. In what areas of life do you need endurance right now?
2. Can you think of times when God used pain to promote spiritual growth?
3. What happens when we try to take a "shortcut" to get out of a difficult situation?

REMOVED, COVERED, GONE FOREVER

Blessed is he whose transgressions are forgiven, whose sins are covered. Blessed is the man whose sin the Lord does not count against him and in whose spirit is no deceit.

PSALM 32:1–2

There is bad news and good news in the gospel.

Psalm 32 is part of David's confession to God after his terrible sin with Bathsheba. He wrote while his hands were still red with the blood of Uriah the Hittite. At first, he tried to "cover" his own sin by pretending it didn't happen. But that brought him only agony, pain, and overwhelming guilt.

Eventually he came to his senses and confessed everything to God. In Romans 4:7–8 the apostle Paul quoted these verses to demonstrate what God's forgiveness means.

What happens to your sin when you trust Jesus Christ as Savior?

First, it is forgiven. "Blessed are [they] whose transgressions are forgiven." The word means to "carry away." It has the idea of physical removal from one location to another. When God forgives you, He removes your sins from you and takes them so far away you will never be able to find them again.

Second, it is covered. "Whose sins are covered." The word means to "cover so completely that it can never be uncovered again." The picture relates to the high priest's sprinkling of the blood of a sacrifice on the yearly Day of Atonement. By sprinkling the blood on the mercy seat, the high priest was acting out a picture of the bloody death of Jesus Christ that would happen hundreds of years later.

The message is clear: *The blood of Jesus is so powerful that it completely covers all your sins*. All means all. If you have trusted Christ, your sins are covered—yesterday, today, tomorrow, and forever.

Third, your sins are not counted against you any longer. "Blessed is the man whose sin the Lord does not count against him." The verb comes from the realm of accounting where accounts are credited or debited. In this context, it means once you trust Christ, your sin will never be counted against you. God will not credit your sin to your account. Why? Because your sin is now "credited" to Christ's account, and His righteousness is now "credited" to your account.

Think of what is being said here. Your sins are forgiven. That's total removal. Your sins are covered. That's total covering. Your sins are not counted against you. That's total disappearance.

There is bad news and good news in the gospel. The bad news is that you are a sinner desperately in need of forgiveness. The good news is that through Christ all your sins can be forgiven forever.

Christians believe in the forgiveness of sins through the blood of Jesus Christ. Apart from Jesus, God has no other plan, and you have no other hope.

Father, I praise You for removing my sin so completely that it can never be used against me. Thank You for Jesus, who was made sin for me that I might be made the righteousness of God in Him. Amen.

1. What evidence of sin do you see in your own life?
2. How have you experienced God's forgiveness?
3. Do you agree that apart from Jesus Christ, God has no other plan of salvation?

NO MORE BLAMING OTHERS

Then I acknowledged my sin to you
and did not cover up my iniquity. I said,
"I will confess my transgressions to the Lord*"*
and you forgave the guilt of my sin.

PSALM 32:5

Confession may be good for the soul,
but it's not an easy step to take.

Psalm 32 shows us what happens when we take courage to admit our wrongdoing and cry out to God for His mercy. Note the key phrase: "I … did not cover up my iniquity." You can cover up—and live riddled with inner guilt—or you can come clean with God and be made clean inside and out.

Some people would rather cover up than clean up. There is a reason we're so good at the blame game. We make excuses because excuse-making is in our family tree. It's part of our spiritual bloodstream. When we pass the buck, we're only doing what our ancestors did.

Let's roll the tape backward to the Garden of Eden and focus our lens right after Adam and Eve have eaten the forbidden fruit. To the untrained eye, it still looks like Paradise. Adam has just eaten the fruit, and a silly, guilty grin slides across his face. He knows he has done something wrong, but he has no idea what will happen next.

Sin first brings shame. And with shame comes the disgrace of being uncovered. Then a strange sound of footsteps. Who could it be? It's the Lord walking in the garden in the cool of the day. Instinctively (and I use that word carefully), Adam and Eve hide themselves. Why? Who told them to hide? No one had to tell them anything. Their guilty consciences condemned them. Disobedience is now bearing its bitter fruit. Where once they enjoyed unbroken fellowship with God, now sin has separated them from their Creator.

But the truth is about to come out. "Have you eaten from the tree that I commanded you not to eat from?" "The woman You put here with me—she gave me some fruit from the tree, and I ate it." That's a classic piece of buck-passing. Blame it on the woman. If that doesn't work, blame it on God. Minimize your guilt by making someone else look bad.

That explains many things:

- It tells us the tendency to blame others is deeply ingrained in human nature.
- It tells us that, left to ourselves, we will do anything to avoid taking personal responsibility for our actions.
- It tells us that blaming others is often nothing more than a subtle twisting of the truth in order to take the heat off ourselves.
- It tells us that without a deep working of the grace of God within us, we will do exactly what Adam and Eve did.

The lesson is clear. Stop blaming others, and you can begin to grow in the Lord.

Lord, I pray to be set free from the need to blame others for my own foolish actions. Amen.

1. Do you agree that honest confession is good for the soul?
2. Why, then, is it so hard to do?
3. Are you still blaming other people for your problems?

ENHANCING GOD'S REPUTATION IN THE WORLD

Glorify the Lord with me;
let us exalt his name together.
PSALM 34:3

The great Puritan preacher Thomas Watson called glory "the sparkling of the Deity."

What precisely does it mean to glorify God? The particular word translated "glorify" in this verse is sometimes translated by words such as "magnify," "exalt," "pile high," and "make grow." It has within it the concept of increasing the size of something. In this context, it means recognizing who God really is and honoring Him for what He has done. You glorify someone when you recognize his true identity and the true worth of his accomplishments.

When our boys were young, we took them on a short vacation to visit relatives in Lexington, Kentucky. During an afternoon trip to a miniature golf course, we noticed an older gentleman with his grandchildren on another part of the course. "Do you know who that is?" someone asked. We didn't. "He was the governor of Kentucky." "You're just making that up." But it was true. The older gentleman turned out to be a distinguished former governor of Kentucky. Our opinion changed instantly from disinterest to great respect.

The most common Old Testament word for *glory* means to treat something as heavy or weighty in nature. The word was used in Genesis 31 for animals heavy-laden with gold. The word also refers to the shining light of God's presence. That glory was the cloud by day and the fiery pillar by night that led the people of God through the wilderness. Later it was the light that filled the tabernacle and the temple. Exodus 24:17 tells us God's glory was like a consuming fire on the top of Mount Sinai.

When we pass into the New Testament, we encounter a Greek word *doxa*, from which we get the English word doxology. This word has the idea of honor, dignity, and reputation. That last word—reputation—brings us very close to the meaning of "glory" in Psalm 34:3. I remember hearing Dr. Charles Ryrie explain that God's glory is His reputation in the world. To live for God's glory means to live so that God's reputation is enhanced, not diminished.

That leads me to a critical thought. In one sense you cannot diminish God's glory. It exists forever because God is eternal. To paraphrase C. S. Lewis, you cannot diminish God's glory any more than a madman can diminish the sun merely by scribbling "darkness" on the walls on his cell.

However, you can cause others to see God's glory or dismiss it entirely by the personal choices you make every day. We glorify God by remembering who He is and what great things He has done for us. As we do that, His reputation in the world is enhanced.

Lord Jesus, I pray to be the kind of person who makes it easy for others to believe in You. Amen.

1. Why did God leave His earthly reputation in the hands of His children?
2. What difference does that make for you?
3. Name three practical ways you can glorify God this week.

WHY JESUS WENT TO THE CROSS

How priceless is your unfailing love!
Both high and low among men find
refuge in the shadow of your wings.

PSALM 36:7

Unfailing love sounds amazing, doesn't it?

Think of a world in which promises are always kept, and the good of others rules every personal relationship. Such a world seems like a dream compared to this poor fallen world of broken promises and broken hearts. No wonder the psalmist called God's unfailing love "priceless." How much we all long for, that love—and how much we would gladly pay to experience it.

What we long for, God has provided in the gift of His Son, the Lord Jesus Christ. This is the "indescribable" gift of 2 Corinthians 9:15, the final proof of God's loving nature. Because God so loved the world, He sent Jesus to be our Savior.

But that raises a profound question: How did Jesus love the world that He came to save? How was His love demonstrated? The answer goes something like this. He loved the world with total vulnerability. He gave Himself so completely that the world turned against Him. He loved the world so much that He was beaten, mocked, bruised, abused, hated, reviled, slandered, and insulted. In the end, the very world He came to save turned against Him. Finally, they nailed Him to the cross.

We know that. We've heard it for years. But there's a deeper point here. Jesus had the power to stop people from hurting Him, and He chose not to use it. He didn't have to take the abuse. He didn't have to allow the mockery. As the song says, "He could have called ten thousand angels to destroy the world and set Him free." That was His prerogative. He was the Son of God. All the power of the universe was at His disposal. One word and a legion of angels would be dispatched to His aid.

But He chose not to do it. That's how He loved the world—with total vulnerability. He loved the world so much He was willing to be killed for the world He loved. The Pharisees thought they had outwitted Him, but they could do nothing without His consent.

I came across this beautiful statement that summarizes what unfailing love means:

> I gave God a million reasons not to love me,
> but none of them changed His mind.

How does Jesus love us? With total, self-sacrificing, vulnerable, and unfailing love. No wonder men and women find refuge under the wings of a God whose love is as vast as an ocean.

O Lord, how magnificent is Your love toward me. Thank You for loving me when I was still a sinner and far from You. Amen.

1. In what way does Jesus "prove" the unfailing love of God?
2. Why didn't Jesus use the power at His disposal to come down from the cross?
3. What does that tell you about the nature of His love?

LEARNING TO WALK IN THE LIGHT

For with you is the fountain of life;
in your light we see light.
PSALM 36:9

Light comes from light—never from the darkness.

This verse contains a hugely important principle for the spiritual life. It tells us that light comes from God and that only as we walk in His light will we see the light.

Let's apply this to the spiritual struggles we all face every day. What starts with a fleeting thought, if not immediately resisted, progresses into action, which leads to sin, which results in death (James 1:13–15). Don't ever let anyone tell you that temptation is wrong.

Temptation isn't wrong; it's normal. If you're not ever tempted, you're already dead!

Each temptation of life brings you face-to-face with a moral choice. Either you give in, or you stand your ground and say no. Each time you give in—even a little bit—you grow weaker, and each time you resist—even when you resist a small temptation—you grow stronger.

A friend came to see me with news that after many years of struggle, she had finally turned the corner in her battle against a debilitating addiction. I told her an illustration that has been very helpful to me. Every day we make hundreds of decisions—most of them very small. We decide what to wear, which way to drive to work, when to go to lunch, and which phone call to return first.

Many of the decisions we make are either a step into the darkness or a step into the light. I told my friend that each day she would face a thousand tiny decisions, and each one would either lead her back into the darkness or toward the light of life. I also reminded her that she hadn't gotten where she was overnight. It took thousands of tiny decisions to get there, and it would take thousands of tiny decisions to get out. But each day, as she took tiny steps toward the light, she would move slowly toward a brand-new life. I promised her that one day, after thousands of tiny steps in the right direction, she would wake up surrounded by the light of God on every side.

A few months later, she wrote me a wonderful note telling me how marvelously her life had changed in the last ten months. She lives and walks in the light of God's love every day. Bit by bit her life has been transformed.

It is nothing short of a miracle. She has discovered the fountain of life, and in His light, she has seen the light. Light comes from light—never from the darkness.

Giver of all light, show me the path
I should take and then give me the
strength to take the next step. Amen.

1. "Light comes from light." What does that phrase mean?
2. What "small steps toward the light" do you need to take today?
3. Thank God for the progress you have made already.

THE BULLDOG AND THE SKUNK

Be still before the Lord and wait patiently for him.

PSALM 37:7

Not all hills are worth dying on.

We all know this is true, but it is a lesson we learn over and over. Sometimes we fight over things that don't matter and waste lots of time and emotional energy with very little to show for it. One of the secrets to a successful life is learning over time which hills matter and which ones don't. Every great general knows you have to pick your battles carefully. You can't fight over every hill or you'll win the battle but lose the war.

There is no easy way to learn this lesson. Everything seems important, vital, crucial, and non-negotiable when we are young. As we get older, we discover that many things that once occupied our time don't matter much in the long run. Perhaps it is a blessing that comes with the aging process. At a certain point in life, you don't have the time, strength, or energy to get involved in every little squabble. So, you decide what matters and what doesn't, and if you're like most people, you end up with a relatively short list of things that matter and a much longer list of things that don't.

A friend passed along a saying that seemed very much on point. "A bulldog can beat a skunk, but is it worth the fight?" If we're laying down bets, I'll put my money on the bulldog every time. But he'll end up smelling like a skunk even if he wins.

What is the point of all this? My mind is drawn to the words of David in Psalm 37:7, "Be still before the Lord and wait patiently for Him; do not fret when men succeed in their ways, when they carry out their wicked schemes."

"Fret" is an old English word that speaks of an unsettled heart. The fretful believer is tossed and turned by circumstances he cannot control. God's solution is simple: 1) Be still before the Lord. That means what it says. Don't take matters into your own hands. 2) Wait patiently for Him. Give God time to work. Chuck Swindoll says that waiting is the hardest discipline of the Christian life. I agree wholeheartedly. We live in a "can-do" society where the people who get ahead are those who "make it happen" no matter what it takes.

Here's a simple application. When you are churning on the inside about things you can't control, don't give in to the temptation to take matters in your own hands. Get alone with God and do nothing. That's right. Just do nothing. Wait on Him.

Or you can be like a bulldog and jump into the fray. But even if you win the battle, you may end up smelling like a skunk.

Lord Jesus, give me wisdom to know when to fight and when to wait on You. Give me grace to trust in the midst of turmoil. Amen.

1. Which hills are you fighting on right now?
2. How can you know when to fight and when to wait on the Lord?
3. Why is it so hard to give up control to the Lord?

MEEKNESS IS NOT WEAKNESS

But the meek will inherit the land and enjoy great peace.

PSALM 37:11

Are you a meek person?

It's hard to answer that question because the word *meek* does not have a positive connotation in our culture. It suggests many things, none of which are very appealing. If you tell someone you think he is meek, he will probably not take it as a compliment. In fact, he will probably think you are implying something negative about his character.

A quick check of the thesaurus bears this out. Here are some listed synonyms for *meek*: humble, docile, mild, calm, gentle, peaceful, tame, submissive, soft, spineless, passive, and broken. Some of those words are positive; others are not. Another source lists the following phrases as illustrative of meekness: "to eat dirt," "to lick the dust," "to cringe like a dog," "to take it on the chin."

That graphically illustrates the problem. Just try sticking some of those words and phrases in the third beatitude (Matt. 5:5) and see what you get:

"Blessed are the spineless, for they will inherit the earth." It doesn't sound right, does it?

Or how about, "Blessed are those who cringe like a dog." It's hard to imagine Jesus (or anyone else) saying that.

It's no wonder we don't want to be called meek. I wouldn't either if that's what the word really means. None of us likes to be bullied. We'd all rather be loved. We tend to value tough, strong, assertive leaders.

The biblical concept of meekness means having your power under God's control. During a radio interview, I was asked to explain meekness as it applies to being a Christian man in today's world. Many men would not feel complimented if someone called them "meek." Yet the interviewer pointed out that Jesus used that very word to describe Himself in Matthew 11:29 (KJV). It seems to me that if Jesus felt comfortable calling Himself "meek" (or "gentle" in some translations, including the NIV), we shouldn't have a big problem with it.

Jesus was no pushover.

The same Jesus who embraced the children also took a whip and cleaned out the temple. Say what you will about it, but don't call Him a sissy. When He confronted sin, He was gentle like a tornado is gentle. But He could be tender and forgiving when the moment called for it.

Gentleness is not weakness. It is our power under God's control. It is the ability to help the hurting while confronting evil whenever necessary. That's a tough combination, but our Lord pulled it off without a hitch.

Holy Spirit, make me like Jesus that my power might be fully under God's control. Amen.

1. When you think of the word *meek*, what images come to mind?
2. Is your power under your control, under God's control, or out of control?
3. Would your friends use the word *meek* to describe you?

HOPE FOR STRAYING SAINTS

If the Lord delights in a
man's way, he makes his steps firm;
though he stumble, he will not fall,
for the Lord upholds him with his hand.

PSALM 37:23–24

Direction makes the difference.

I ate lunch with a man who told me how he came to Christ just a few years before. He said that after his conversion, someone asked him to explain what being a Christian means. What difference does Jesus make once He becomes both Lord and Savior? His answer was profound: "I've learned that I can sin, but I can't enjoy it like I used to."

You can still sin and enjoy it for a while, but not forever. God will not let His children enjoy the pleasures of sin indefinitely. Sooner or later, He steps in and brings His wandering sons and daughters back home to Him.

If we graphed the spiritual experience of most Christians, it would move up and down, up and down, up and down—but always moving in a generally upward direction. At any given moment, the graph of your life may show you relatively up or relatively down spiritually. You may be down for a long time, but if you know Jesus, you will eventually start moving up again. I draw two conclusions from this:

1. Direction makes the difference.
2. True believers move toward heaven.

It is possible to fall into grievous sin, but that's not where we belong, and we will not stay there forever. *If you are a Christian, you won't be comfortable living in sin.* The direction of your life will be away from sin and toward Jesus Christ. It has been said that "I would rather be one foot away from hell heading toward heaven than one foot away from heaven heading toward hell."

Direction makes the difference.

Some people are saved one foot from hell. God turns them around at the very brink of the pit. When they are saved, they still have the smell of brimstone in their clothing. That's why new Christians sometimes look and act pretty rough. They've been snatched from the flames. Some of those same people will still look rough after five or ten years. That's OK because they started so low. You don't judge people by where they are now, but by where they've come from.

Take heart in God's restoring grace. The only thing that matters is to keep moving in the right direction. Sometimes we fly like an eagle. Sometimes we run with stallions. Sometimes we walk in victory. And sometimes we're just stumbling upward. I love that phrase—stumbling upward. That's the testimony of nearly all God's saints—we're stumbling upward toward heaven.

Father, I praise You for grace so great that it goes beyond my sin, finds me when I have fallen, picks me up, and sets my feet back on the road to heaven. Amen.

1. Do you agree true saints of God will move toward heaven?
2. What is the direction of your life at this moment?
3. Can you think of a time when God's grace restored you when you stumbled?

GOD BLESSES GENEROUS GIVERS

I was young and now I am old, yet I have never seen the righteous forsaken or their children begging bread. They are always generous and lend freely; their children will be blessed.

PSALM 37:25–26

Here is an amazing truth.

God promises to bless generous givers. He even promises to bless their children. That's reason enough to give until the day you die.

Most of us have a bit of built-in selfishness as part of our nature. In a day of high prices, unemployment, and much uncertainty, it's easy to focus all your energy on building up your net worth and to forget about people.

When you give money to a worthy cause, cook a meal for a friend, give a bag of groceries, anonymously slip a twenty-dollar bill in an envelope and mail it, or move to meet the real needs around you, you are doing exactly what God expects—you are supplying the needs of the saints.

I've never forgotten something that happened when I pastored a small church in the Los Angeles area many years ago. One young couple in that church experienced a long string of setbacks: unemployment, sickness, losing their home, and family problems of every description. At one point the wife became pregnant and was expecting twins. Late in the pregnancy, complications developed, and one of the babies died before delivery.

At that moment, the husband got sick and couldn't work. The roof caved in around them. The church rallied to their cause, raised money on their behalf, bought groceries, prepared meals, and helped pay the rent. Church members helped take care of the children and did the chores around the house until the family could get on their feet.

Sometime later, after the crisis had passed, the wife sent the church a note that said something like this: "I thank God for all you have done. God used you to help us out when we really needed help. I'm glad to be part of a church that cares."

Our giving not only meets physical needs but also raises a great chorus of thanksgiving before the throne of God. When we give to help others, they know we do it in the name of Jesus of Nazareth, who went about doing good, and they glorify God, who made our giving possible.

How does it work? When we give as Christians, a divine name tag is attached to every dollar we give, every meal we cook, and every piece of clothing we donate. Our giving reflects on our heavenly Father and enhances His reputation in the world.

O Father, You have given me all that I possess. I pray now to be given the gift of a generous spirit. Amen.

1. Can you think of a time when you were on the receiving end of generous giving by other Christians?
2. What did you learn from that experience?
3. Would the people who know you best call you a generous person?

MARTIN LUTHER'S COMMENT

I confess my iniquity;
I am troubled by my sin.
PSALM 38:18

No one is sinless in this life.

It isn't often that I have breakfast with a church historian, but it happened recently, and I learned something very useful. We shared bagels and cream cheese and discussed the theology of the Reformation—his specialty. During our conversation, he related a famous quote by Martin Luther. It is, he said, central to Luther's view of the spiritual life.

It is one simple sentence filled with meaning: "The whole Christian life is a life of repentance."

As I considered those words, I could not find anything to quarrel with. But the words seem strange to modern ears. Repentance is not a concept we like to think about. It implies guilt, which we would rather not admit, and it speaks of changing our ways and reforming our habits, which in the best of times is not easy to do. Perhaps some of us have been taught that repentance happens only once—the moment you become a Christian.

Although some people would like to deny this, both the Bible and common sense unite to teach us that as long as we live in this fallen world, we will struggle with sin to one degree or another. But not just the fallen world is a problem;

our fallen nature also remains with us. In some sense our basic sinful nature remains a part of us even after we are born again.

In Luther's words once again, we are "simultaneously justified and sinful," righteous before God because of His imputed righteousness but sinful in ourselves.

Try as we might, we will never be completely rid of sin in this life. The fact that sin remains with us till the day we die should not discourage us in the least. In the words of Anselm of Canterbury, one of the greatest of all the medieval theologians, "You have not yet considered how great your sin is."

Is there anything positive from the believer's continual struggle with sin? Yes. First, our struggles develop humility and kill pride. Second, they create a deep desire for the grace of God. Third, our struggles teach us the truth of John 15:5, that apart from a living relationship with Jesus Christ, we have no power within us to defeat sin and live in righteousness.

Repentance starts when we say, "Lord, You were right all along, and I was wrong." But that should not be hard for us to say because when we sin, we are always wrong, and God is always right.

Lord Jesus, I long to be delivered from my bondage to sin. Grant that I might emerge victorious by Your power. Amen.

1. Do you agree with Martin Luther's comment that "The whole Christian life is a life of repentance"?
2. Why is sinless perfection impossible in this life?
3. Why would God allow us to be simultaneously justified and sinful?

LIFE IS SHORT!

Show me, O Lord, my life's
end and the number of my days;
let me know how fleeting my life is.
PSALM 39:4

Life is fleeting for all of us.

A woman in Florida was diagnosed with pancreatic cancer. Knowing she had only a few months to live, she penned her own obituary which was published after she died. With wit and a cheerful spirit, she recounted her life story. But she summed it all up in one sentence: "I was born, I blinked, and it was over."

Martin Luther said we should live with the day of our death constantly before our eyes. As I ponder that thought, the words of a famous hymn come to mind:

Time, like an ever-rolling stream,
Bears all its sons away;
They fly forgotten, as a dream
Dies at the opening day.

Most of us don't have the advantage of knowing when we will die. James 4:14 reminds us life itself is like a vapor that appears for a moment and then vanishes away. Anyone who has ever blown hot breath on a cold windowpane knows you have to work fast to write your name in the vapor before it disappears. That's your life—all 70 or 80 or 90 years of it. It's a vapor that begins to disappear the moment you are born.

We aren't here very long. I ran across a website with this motto: "On a long enough timeline, the survival rate for everyone drops to zero." British playwright George Bernard Shaw wryly observed, "The statistics on death are quite impressive. One out of one people die."

Go to the cemetery and look at any headstone. There is a name, two dates, and a dash. That's what you get when you die: a little "–" to summarize your earthly existence.

No one lives forever. We are born, we live 30 or 40 or 50 or 60 years. If we are strong and healthy and blessed by God, we may live to be 80 or even 90. Some people live to be 100. But it doesn't matter how long you live because eventually everyone dies. We're all terminal. The only difference is that some of us know it, and the rest of us act like we're going to be here forever. If you live each day as if it might be your last, one day you will be right.

Sportscaster Dan Patrick once remarked about an injured player, "He's listed as day to day, but, then again, aren't we all?" "So teach us to number our days," said the psalmist, "that we may apply our hearts unto wisdom," (KJV). How true.

Lord, help me to enjoy each day
as a gift from You. Amen.

1. How long do you expect to live?
2. How long do you want to live?
3. Have you "numbered your days" yet?

MISSIONARY EYES

Blessed is he who has regard for the weak;
the Lord delivers him in times of trouble.

PSALM 41:1

Jesus is never tolerant of sin
but always willing to forgive it.

The letter was short, to-the-point, and refreshingly honest:

> I felt I should tell you a little bit of a story in hopes it might help someone else. Whenever I tell others about my rough road back to Christ from non-Christian relationships, the one question I am always asked is, "What would have helped make your road back a little easier?" My answer is, during my time of spiritual loneliness, if I had had a sister in Christ seek me out and tell me, "I've been there, I love you, and I can help you find your way back to Jesus," perhaps I could have been spared a lot more pain than having to discover the answers on my own.

She then adds this PS. "Jesus is never tolerant of sin but always willing to forgive it. If my experience can help someone else, feel free to use this information."

I certainly am glad to pass it on because it is truly encouraging. And it reminds us we will all grow stronger as we lean on each other. If you're having a hard time keeping your head above water, tell someone else.

Don't fight the battle all by yourself. Let the Lord minister to you through the resources of the body of Christ.

Check out the Bible verse at the top of this entry. God blesses those who care for the weak. Are you in need of God's blessing right now? Find a brother or sister in need and give him or her a helping hand. So many believers struggle because they try to handle their problems alone. But God never meant you should walk through the lonely valley by yourself. Hebrews 10:24 says, "Let us consider how we may spur one another on toward love and good deeds."

Think of the people you know right now who are going through a hard time. Make a list. Now ask yourself how many others are going through a hard time you don't know about. The truth is, we all struggle some of the time and some of us struggle most of the time.

When people ask me what they can do to help others, my answer is always the same. *Start where you are*. Open your eyes to see the hurting faces you meet every day. Our greatest problem is not that we won't help hurting people; it's that all too often we don't even see them in the first place.

Sometimes a positive word can save a life. Desperate people want to know someone cares about them. Open your eyes. Better yet, ask God to open them for you. Pray for "missionary eyes" to see the needs of those you meet today. You can help someone get better if you will look closely at the faces you see every day.

Holy Spirit, give me missionary eyes to see the hurting people all around me. I pray to be a load lifter for a weary pilgrim today. Amen.

1. Have you ever felt like the writer of that note, wishing for someone to help you get back on track?
2. Do you know someone who is in that position right now?
3. What could you do to help the person out?

A THIEF LOOSE IN THE CHURCH

All my enemies whisper together against me;
they imagine the worst for me.
PSALM 41:7

There is a thief who lives inside most churches.

He (or she) is a thief because he steals someone else's good name. "Psssst … Have you heard the latest?" "Did you know that Sally and Bill are splitting up?" "She never intended to pay the money back." "He said he was sick, but I'll bet he was just playing golf." "I'm glad she lost her job. She needed to get some humility." "Those Johnson kids are the worst children in church. I think the middle one will probably end up in Congress … or in jail … or both."

On and on it goes. In politics the level of public discourse has reached an all-time low. We seem fixated on the salacious details of the private lives of our leaders. Each candidate perfects his sleazy attack ads on the opposition, carefully twisting the facts and slightly distorting the truth until a negative image is drawn. We say we don't like it, but politicians wouldn't use those ads if we didn't pay attention to them.

No church is immune to the problem of gossip, including the church where I am the pastor. People love to talk, and they love to talk about other people. This is an undeniable fact of human nature. How do you know when you've "crossed the line" from conversation to gossip? When truth is sacrificed, you've crossed the line. But you can tell the truth and still gossip if you intend to make another person look bad.

Just remember this. You're guilty of stealing their good name when you gossip about other people. You are guilty of robbery just as much as the mugger who holds you up on the street. And you aren't any less guilty in God's eyes. No, you are worse because you do it in God's house, and you attack God's children.

Shakespeare said it well in these famous words from Othello:

> Who steals my purse, steals trash;
> 'tis something, nothing;
> 'Twas mine, 'tis his, and has been slave to thousands;
> But he that filches from me my good name
> Robs me of that which not enriches him,
> And makes me poor indeed.

If any other evidence needs to be mentioned, remember gossip is listed in Romans 1:29–31—along with murder—as one mark of a depraved life. There is such a thing as a gossiping thief—a category that may apply to you more than you think.

Here's a test. Just go to three close friends this week and ask them: Do you think I have a tendency to gossip? You might be surprised at the answers you get.

O Lord, may my words be used only to build up and never to tear down. Amen.

1. What is the essential difference between talking about others and harmful gossip?
2. Have you ever been harmed by the gossiping words of others?
3. Ask God to create sensitivity in your heart so that you will think twice before you gossip about others.

SHOUT!

Clap your hands, all you nations;
shout to God with cries of joy.

PSALM 47:1

Worship is to be the central act of life.

Since it is supposed to be the main thing we do, worship is not simply coming to church. It is something we actively do with our bodies and entire selves. The Bible mentions things like singing, clapping, shouting, laughing, kneeling, saying "amen," speaking, sitting in silence, chanting, praying, lifting up the hands, lying prostrate on the floor, beating the chest, crying, blessing God and others, joining hands, singing in the choir, listening to the choir, playing cymbals, horns, bells, pipes, trumpets, and even dancing.

Christianity is a singing faith. Martin Luther wrote these wise words about the value of music in the Christian life:

> I have no use for cranks who despise music, because it is a gift of God. Music drives away the devil and makes people happy; they forget thereby all wrath, unchastity, arrogance, and the like. Next after theology I give to music the highest place and the greatest honor.

There have been many occasions when I came to church on Sunday morning feeling weak and tired. Perhaps it was because of a busy week or perhaps I was carrying a particular burden. Sometimes my mind would be going in a thousand different directions. Then the worship service would begin. It might be with the pipe organ playing "Come, Thou Almighty King," or it might be with the worship band leading "In Christ Alone." Or it might be singing "Like a River Glorious" or "It Is Well with My Soul" or "Guide Me, O Thou Great Jehovah," or perhaps it was a new worship chorus I was learning for the first time. As the congregation worshiped, my mind cleared, my doubts departed, my worries receded, my faith swelled, my heart was lifted to heaven, and when the time came to preach, the Holy Spirit came in great power. This has happened so many times I cannot believe it was by chance.

Warren Wiersbe defines worship as "the believer's adoring response of all that he is, mind, emotions, will and body, to all that God is and says and does." That definition doesn't mention a pipe organ or a contemporary praise band. It doesn't say anything about drums or a robed choir. Nor does it touch the burning issue of choruses versus stately hymns. We get hung up on those outward manifestations when the Bible tells us worship involves our response of all we are to all God has revealed Himself to be.

The application of this is very simple:

- Let the pastors sing!
- Let the elders sing!
- Let the adults sing!
- Let the children sing!

When God Himself grips your soul, every day will be Sunday, and worship will be as natural as breathing.

Lord God, teach me to worship with all my heart and all my soul all the time. Amen.

1. How do you define worship?
2. Do you find it easier to worship in church on Sunday morning than during the week?
3. How would today be different if you worshiped God all day long?

TRUTH FROM THE INSIDE OUT

Surely you desire truth in the inner parts; you teach me wisdom in the inmost place.

PSALM 51:6

It had been a messy affair.

But now things seemed to be going well. After all, who could fault a king for indulging his fantasies? That's what kings do. One night, you go out for a stroll, you see a beautiful woman, you want her, you send for her, and she comes to you. It's as simple as that. Kings have been doing that sort of thing since the beginning of time.

Whatever the king wants, the king gets.

That's the backstory of David and Bathsheba.

So he took a walk one evening, saw Bathsheba, and the whole course of his life changed. To be sure, he never intended to commit adultery and murder, but that's where it ended up.

You can read the story for yourself in 2 Samuel 11.

Then came the time for David to do the hardest thing anyone can ever do, to look in the mirror and say, "I have sinned." *Those may be the three hardest words in the English language*. No one wants to say, "I have sinned." We would rather do anything than say that. But there is no getting right until we admit how badly we have done wrong.

All sin is treason against the Almighty. Until we grasp that, until we see it and feel it, until we confess it, we cannot be forgiven.

When David confessed his sin to the Lord, he said that God desires "truth in the inner parts" (Psalm 51:6). *That means God wants truth from the inside out.*

Would you like to be set free?

Would you like to be forgiven?

Would you like to see the power of the Holy Spirit released in your life?

Would you like to see God do something miraculous in the relationships that matter most to you? *It can happen, but you must tell the truth from the inside out.*

It reminds me of the famous Jack Nicholson scene in the movie *A Few Good Men* where he says to Tom Cruise, "You want the truth?" When Cruise replies, "Yes, I do," Nicholson shouts in a rage, "You can't handle the truth."

The truly free people are not those who do whatever they want. Truly free people have dared to tell the painful truth about themselves, and in the process, they have been set free.

When David cried out for God's mercy, he acknowledged the true source of the problem—and where the healing must begin. As long as we lie to ourselves, we can never get better, and God cannot teach us wisdom that leads to true freedom.

Would you like to be set free? It begins when you tell the truth from the inside out.

Lord God, give me the courage to face the truth about myself so that I can be set free. Amen.

1. Why is knowing the truth never enough to produce spiritual growth?
2. Name some ways people hide from painful truth.
3. In what areas of your life are you lying to yourself (or making silly excuses)?

DON'T TAKE YOUR HOLY SPIRIT AWAY!

Do not cast me from your presence
or take your Holy Spirit from me.

PSALM 51:11

It is sometimes said that no Christian should ever feel the need to pray this prayer of David, but I wonder if that is correct.

Clearly David feared being cast away by God and losing the Holy Spirit. The big question is not, "What does this verse mean for us?" But rather, "What did it mean for David? What was he thinking and feeling when he prayed this prayer?"

This is not David before he met the Lord. This is David, the man of God, who has an unclean heart. This is not David the unbeliever. This is David the man after God's own heart.

He is a man of God with an unclean heart.

Because of his sin, he has lost God's blessing.

When Charles Spurgeon preached on this verse, he said these are fitting words for any Christian who has fallen into sin. Small sins are often more dangerous than big ones because big ones startle us into repentance, but just like the frog in the boiling kettle of water, we may gradually become so used to sin that it ceases to bother us. Many small sins may produce a worse effect than one big sin.

Then Spurgeon asks a long series of questions, which I have paraphrased and updated:

- Have we taken God's grace for granted?
- Has our love for God grown cold?
- Are we careless about prayer?
- Have we slowly grown lukewarm in our Christian faith?
- Do we love the world too much?
- Do we harbor a root of bitterness?
- Have we spoken unkindly of other Christians?
- Are we careless in our words?
- Have we become spiritually cold?

What an encouragement this ought to be to all of us. Are there any Christians who have grieved the Lord again and again? Any adulterers? Any murderers? Any slanderers? Any liars? Any lawbreakers?

If you feel the pain of your sin, you must know the Lord. *The guilt you feel is a severe mercy God gives to His erring children*. Your tears are signs of life within. Your pain and your shame and your frustration are signs you are a true child of God.

There are times when a Christian must pray like a sinner. Spurgeon says it very well:

> The lower down we get the better. I frequently find that I cannot pray as a minister; I find that I cannot sometimes pray as an assured Christian, but I bless God I can pray as a sinner. I begin again with, "God, be merciful to me, a sinner," and by degrees rise up again to faith, and onward to assurance.

If you have been sinning, do not be ashamed to pray like a sinner. That's not a bad place to start.

Lord Jesus, I dare not go one more day without Your blessing. Show me what needs to change so that Your Spirit may fill me once again. Amen.

1. Do you agree the Holy Spirit may remove His power from a believer's life?
2. How would we know when that happens?
3. How would you answer Spurgeon's nine questions?

SPEAKING THE TRUTH IN LOVE

Then I will teach transgressors your ways,
and sinners will turn back to you.

PSALM 51:13

What have you learned from your mistakes?

That's what David pondered after his foolish affair with Bathsheba that led to the murder of Uriah the Hittite.

Can anything good come out of something so evil? The answer is yes, if we are willing to learn what God wants to teach us. In Psalm 51:13, David vows he will use his experience to cause sinners to return to the Lord. This is the heart of evangelism—telling others what Christ has done for us. Until we have personally experienced God's pardoning grace, the gospel is only a theoretical message to us.

But let a person declare how God rescued him in his moment of helpless desperation, let him speak openly of how he despaired of ever finding peace with God. Let him tell how Jesus found him, lifted him up, forgave his sins, gave him a new life, and set his feet in a new direction—let him tell that from his heart, and people will listen, because there is no testimony like the simple truth of a changed life.

Converted sinners make the best preachers because they know the truth of what they are saying.

Consider how Jesus dealt with people. He loved sinners and felt comfortable around them. He routinely went places and spent time with people in ways that many of us personally wouldn't care to do.

That statement says something about many modern Christians. We fall far short of Christ's compassion for the lost. He welcomed everyone and turned no one away. He encouraged every genuine seeker who crossed His path. And He answered most of their questions—the good and the bad, the honest and the insincere.

But that same Jesus also rebuked the Pharisees, cleared out the temple courtyard with a whip, and repeatedly spoke hard truth to powerful people without the slightest regard for His own safety.

What was He like? John 1:14 tells us He was "full of grace and truth." What a wonderful phrase! He was perfectly balanced between truth and love at all times.

We face the same challenge today: to balance truth and love in all our relationships. We are to know the truth and to walk in love—all the time. If we emphasize only the truth, we risk becoming hard and mean-spirited. That alienates other believers and turns the lost away from Christ. If we emphasize only love, we risk becoming soft and sentimental. That soon leads us to compromise the gospel, excuse sin, and welcome evildoers.

We must speak the truth in love. When we do, we will see sinners converted and transgressors returning to God.

O God, I fall so far short of loving people as Jesus did. Create in me the mind and heart of Christ that I might live and love as He did. Amen.

1. In what ways did Jesus demonstrate a perfect balance between truth and love?
2. Are you more likely to emphasize the truth part or the love part?
3. How has Jesus changed your life in this area?

YOUR ONLY HOPE OF HEAVEN

But as for me, I trust in you.

PSALM 55:23

Was Jesus' death enough?

It happened early in the week. A friend said, "Preach well this Sunday. Someone I love will be in the service. I want my friend to know Jesus." What a tremendous encouragement to a pastor's heart.

All week long I thought about how to end my sermon. The answer came while I was driving home from a hospital visit. I happened to catch a few minutes of an interview with Pastor Erwin Lutzer as he discussed God's plan of salvation. I listened as a woman called with a gripping question. She said all her friends would be surprised if they heard her call, because they all considered her to be a good Christian. But in her heart she had no assurance. She prayed the sinner's prayer every day just to be sure. Her question was simple: "How can I be sure I'm going to heaven?"

Pastor Lutzer gave an excellent answer. "I want you to think about the cross of Christ and what it represents. Do you believe what Jesus did on the cross was enough for your salvation? Or do you think you need to add anything to what Jesus did?"

That's really the central question for all of us to consider. When Jesus died, was His death enough so that there is nothing else you need to do for your own salvation? If the answer is yes, then you can be saved and you can also be sure. If the answer is no, then you can never be sure because you can never do enough.

Thank God the answer is an eternal yes. "Jesus paid it all, all to Him I owe; Sin had left a crimson stain, He washed it white as snow." Can you make the following statements?

- "I believe the Cross was enough for me."
- "I am willing to trust Jesus Christ completely and absolutely!"
- "I want to go to heaven, and I'm trusting Jesus to take me there."
- "I'm trusting my whole life into Jesus' almighty hands."

If you want to be saved, run to the cross of Christ. Lay hold of Jesus by faith. Fix all your hope on Him. Those who trust in Jesus will never be disappointed.

Do you know Jesus? Have you ever met Him personally? His name is the greatest name in all the universe. It doesn't matter who else you know or don't know. You may know leaders, kings, presidents, and potentates, but if you do not know Jesus, you've missed the reason for your existence.

Do you know Him?

Lord Jesus, nothing is more important than knowing You. I pray for deep assurance that I have trusted You as my Savior. Amen.

1. Why is "do you know Him?" the most important question?
2. What is your own answer to that question?
3. Take a moment to pray along the lines suggested in this entry.

A CHOICE, NOT A FEELING

In God, whose word I praise,
in God I trust; I will not be afraid.
What can mortal man do to me?
PSALM 56:4

Can you trust God? Or better:
Can God be trusted?

More and more I am convinced this is the fundamental question of life: "Is God good, and can He be trusted to do what is right?" If the answer is yes, then we can face the worst life has to offer. If the answer is no, then we're no better off than the people who have no faith at all. In fact, if the answer is no or if we're not sure, then we really don't have any faith anyway.

While doing a radio interview for a station in Yakima, Washington, I was asked how I could be so positive and confident when I spoke about God's will. The man asking the question seemed burdened with many cares and difficulties.

My answer went this way: "When my father died many years ago, I came face-to-face with the ultimate unanswerable question of life. I didn't know then why such a good man would have to die at the age of fifty-six, or why he would leave my mother and her four sons without a husband and a father. I had no clue about what God was doing. In the years since then I have learned many things about life, but I confess I still don't understand why my father died. It makes no more sense to me now than it did then.

"I am older and wiser, but in the one question that really matters I have no answers. I have learned since then that faith is a choice you make. Sometimes you choose to believe because of what you see; often you believe in spite of what you can see. Many things remain mysterious and unanswerable as I look to the world around me. But nothing at all makes sense if there is no God or if He is not good. I have chosen to believe because I must believe. I truly have no other choice. If I sound confident, it is only because I have learned through my tears that my only confidence is in God and God alone."

Faith is not a feeling. It's a choice we make moment by moment. Faith rests on the truth that God is who He said He is and will do what He said He would.

God has spoken, and His Word is true. I choose to believe because deep in my soul I have no other choice. As David said, "What can man do to me?" Because I believe, I am not afraid. That's the difference faith makes to a believer.

Eternal God, You alone give meaning and purpose to life. Apart from You, nothing in this world makes sense. Amen.

1. How can you know that God is there, even though you cannot see Him?
2. Do you believe God can be trusted? Why or why not?
3. What gives you the strength to go on when faced with unexplainable tragedy?

A FAINT SOUND ON THE INSIDE

I cry out to God Most High, to God, who fulfills his purpose for me.

PSALM 57:2

Sanctification is God's hammering and sawing in our lives.

These are the words of a man who has been profoundly changed by God:

> Sixteen years ago, I was at the end of my emotional and spiritual rope. One day I got down on my knees and told God to either change me or take me home because I didn't want to live another minute if my life was going to be the same as it had been.
>
> That's when I started to hear the faint sounds of hammering and sawing inside. Over the last sixteen years God has created a whole new person inside this one. That's not visible to most folks. And it wasn't in the twinkling of an eye. But it is a miracle! It is spectacular! And it isn't over yet!
>
> What God has done in my life is more miraculous than if He had grown a new arm or leg to replace an amputated one—because He has grown a whole new

person. He still does miracles! They are spectacular! They are in his time! To God be the glory!

I love one particular sentence in that testimony: "That's when I started to hear the faint sounds of hammering and sawing inside." If you have been a believer for any length of time, you already know about that hammering and sawing in your own life. Theologians have a big word for that. They call it "sanctification." It's the work God does inside the heart of a believer in order to make him into a brand-new person. That leads me to offer a street-level definition of sanctification: It is everything God does in your life and mine to make sure we turn out right.

Sanctification is not some mystical, strange, emotional experience. Whenever you invest in someone's life, you care about how that person turns out. That's why parents care so much and worry so much about their children. They have given their lifeblood, and so it matters almost more than life itself how their children turn out.

Now apply that same truth in the spiritual realm. God has invested in us through the death of His only begotten Son. Sanctification is the divine guarantee that God's investment will not be wasted.

Sanctification, then, is God's commitment to us. We're going to make it. He will personally see to it.

Father, I bless You that I am not what I used to be, though I am not yet everything I want to be. By Your grace I am not yet all I am going to be. Amen.

1. Where have you sensed the "faint sound of hammering and sawing" in your life?
2. What "investment" has God made in His children?
3. What guarantee do we have that He will finish His work in us?

A SOLID FOUNDATION IN A SHAKY WORLD

You have shaken the land and torn it open;
mend its fractures, for it is quaking.
PSALM 60:2

Everything in this world is shakable.

When I lived in California, we had a small tremor one day. It happened while I was driving home from church at lunchtime. Suddenly the car started rocking. I looked outside, and the street was rocking. I was scared to death. To me, an earthquake is the most terrifying natural disaster. If a tornado comes, at least you can head for cover. But what do you do if the very ground on which you stand gives way beneath you? Where do you go then?

But the kingdom of God lasts forever. When the angel Gabriel came to Mary, he said she would give birth to a son who would "reign over the house of Jacob forever; His kingdom will never end" (Luke 1:33).

God desires to establish a kingdom on earth that will last forever. That kingdom will be made up of men and women who have decided to live by God's eternal values.

God's Word is clear: Don't pin your hopes on the world system. It's going down for good. It can't last. It's going to crumble and fall. The whole world and everything in it will be destroyed. If you live for this world, on that day everything you live for will be nothing but dust.

You can live for this world, or you can live for the kingdom of God. The choice is yours.

Jesus has a kingdom.

- He is building it in human hearts around the world.
- Someday He will return and visibly reign on the earth.
- That kingdom will never end.

Some men and women are not like everyone else. They have been gripped by the thought that the kingdom of God is the greatest thing in the world, and that one thought has revolutionized their lives and reoriented their values. Kingdom issues are at stake. That's the only possible explanation for the way they live.

His kingdom will never end. Why would you follow anyone else?

Lord, save me from building my life around things that will one day disappear. Show me the things that will last forever. Amen.

1. Do you agree this world won't last forever?
2. How much of your life is spent dealing with things that will one day disappear?
3. What have you done in the last twenty-four hours that will have eternal significance?

GOD'S ENEMIES WON'T LAST FOREVER

May God arise, may his enemies be scattered;
may his foes flee before him.

PSALM 68:1

God doesn't take it lightly when the people He created turn against Him.

Many of us feel uncomfortable with the notion that God has enemies. If God is a God of love (and He is), how can He have enemies? The answer is that God is not only a God of love but also a God of justice.

Consider these facts:

Fact # 1: God's enemies will be scattered.
Fact # 2: God's enemies don't understand Fact # 1.
Fact # 3: God's people rejoice in Fact # 1.

We may stumble at the word *enemies*. But it's in the Bible. God takes it personally when people turn away from Him. We live in a day when few people will speak of God's anger toward sinners. We risk being called intolerant if we suggest God has any enemies. Yet He does.

God stands up for His own, fights against His enemies, and doesn't bless His opposition. Against the moral relativism of this day, we must plainly say not everyone is going to heaven, not everyone is a child of God, and not everyone will be saved. Many will, but many won't.

Psalm 68:1–2 uses three words to describe what happens to God's enemies.

1. They are *scattered*. (Their power is broken. Their alliances are smashed. Their armies are routed.)
2. They *flee*. (They run from God's judgment, and all their works are destroyed.)
3. They will *perish*. (They suffer in eternal torment in hell.)

In an anything-goes age, Psalm 68 reminds us that when it comes to God, He stays, and His enemies go.

Do we truly believe these solemn words? Do we believe God's enemies will one day be destroyed? Perhaps we should ask the question another way: Do we believe God's enemies will one day perish in everlasting hell? Do these words affect our hearts as we consider the lost people around us?

They are standing on thin ice right now, suspended only by the grace of God. The worst sinners who curse God must use the air He provided to curse His name.

Should these verses not also break our hearts? Should they not sober us, humble us, and force us to our knees? Must we not do everything in our power to save as many people as possible?

If we gloat over the fate of the wicked, if we rejoice in the death of the wicked, then we do not have the heart of God. God takes no pleasure in the death of the wicked. He punishes them, destroys them, and scatters them, but He does it with a broken heart.

Do we have the heart of God even for His enemies?

Lord Jesus, I find it all too easy to hate my enemies and to wish the worst upon them. Teach me to love the people I want to hate so that I might share Your love with them. Amen.

1. Are you uncomfortable with the thought that God has enemies?
2. Who are His enemies today?
3. Take a moment to pray for God's enemies that, through Jesus Christ, they might become His friends.

CURING THE "IF ONLYS" OF LIFE

But may the righteous be glad and rejoice before God; may they be happy and joyful.

PSALM 68:3

Are you happy? Really happy?
Are you satisfied with your life?

Here is the startling truth: If things could make us happy, we'd be in paradise daily. We think "more is better." Is it? It seems the more we have, the less we like it.

Perhaps you've heard the story about the king who fell into a severe depression. Nothing could lift his spirits. His servants tried everything—music, dancing, court jesters, lavish banquets, beautiful flowers—yet nothing seemed to help him.

Finally, an old and wise man came to the king with an unusual piece of advice. "O King, if you can obtain the shirt off the back of a truly happy man, you yourself will be happy." Upon hearing those words, the king ordered his men to search the four corners of the earth and bring him the shirt off the back of a truly happy man. Weeks passed, then months.

Finally, his soldiers returned. "O King, after many days and much searching, we found a truly happy man. But your majesty, the man was not wearing a shirt."

How fitting, how true to life. We think to ourselves,

"If only I had" and then we fill in the blank with our latest dream.

A new house, a new wife, a new set of children, a new job, a new school, a new career, a new church, a new portfolio, a new start in life. Oh, how happy we'd be … if only!

No wonder we're unhappy, discontented, miserable, and we dream so much. Coveting has done its evil work within. It has bored into our soul, eating away our happiness, leaving us empty, frustrated, and angry.

But that raises a question. At what point does legitimate desire become coveting? Coveting occurs either when I desire something I have no right to have (e.g. my neighbor's wife) or when the desire becomes the controlling passion of my life so that I begin to believe my happiness depends on the acquisition of the item itself.

A new house may be nice, but my happiness does not depend on a new house. If it does, then I am coveting it. A new car may help me get around, but it can't be the source of my happiness. If it is, then I am coveting.

The moment I trick myself into thinking, *This [item or goal] is necessary for my happiness in life,* then I have crossed the line into coveting.

David reminds us in Psalm 68:3 of a truth we already know—but often forget: Happy are they who find their happiness in God. They shall be happy indeed.

Lord, do whatever it takes to make me happy in You. If that means making me miserable with the things of this world, so be it. Amen.

1. How happy are you right now?
2. What else do you need to be happy at this moment?
3. What does it mean to you to find happiness in God?

WHEN GOD HIDES HIS FACE

Do not hide your face from your servant;
answer me quickly, for I am in trouble.

PSALM 69:17

This verse raises an interesting question.
Why would God hide His face from His servant?

Why does God seem to disappear in the moment of trouble? Surely the Lord knows how much we need Him.

The answer can be found along these lines: *Often God seems to leave us alone to bring us to the end of our human resources.* As long as we think we can finagle our way out of a crisis, it's easy to think we don't really need God. It is like the woman who, when told by the doctor she should pray, replied, "My soul, is it that bad?" In truth, without God it is always "that bad"; it's just that we don't realize it until the bottom caves in.

There is a second reason God hides Himself. *He does it so that He might be seen only by those with eyes of faith.* The word *hide* can also be translated *veil.* In ancient times kings would put veils before their chambers so that only those who knew the king would find the entrance.

Sometimes God's face is veiled from our sight so that we might exercise our faith in the darkness. Jesus said something similar when asked why He taught so much in parables. Those simple stories were given so that unbelievers would be baffled but His followers would understand.

In a similar vein, the New Testament indicates that after His resurrection, Jesus was seen only by believers. Why? Because unbelievers wouldn't appreciate the fact that He had been raised from the dead.

The third reason brings us to the point of the text. *God often hides Himself so that He might test our motives.* Are we praying simply to get out of trouble, or because we want to glorify God in all that we do? Do we desire an answer to our prayers, or will we be content if the Lord Himself is the answer?

God has ordered the moral universe so that His purposes are advanced as much through suffering as prosperity. This does not make suffering easy, but it does give us a new—and higher—perspective.

Should we, like David, pray for God to answer us speedily in the moment of crisis? Yes, of course. Let us then wait for God to answer—in His own time, in His own way, according to His own will.

Father, thank You for being there even
when I think You are not there. Amen.

1. How do you respond when God answers "no" to your prayers?
2. Can you remember a time when God answered "yes"—but in a completely unexpected way?
3. What does that teach you about God?

WHERE GOD ANSWERS HARD QUESTIONS

When I tried to understand all this, it was oppressive to me till I entered the sanctuary of God; then I understood their final destiny.

PSALM 73:16–17

Why do the wicked prosper?

I love Psalm 73. It has been a personal favorite for as long as I have been reading the Psalms. Written by Asaph (leader of one of the temple choirs), it deals with a question that has troubled the people of God across the centuries: Why do the wicked prosper?

He is not asking why the righteous suffer (as Job does), but his eyes are fixed on a more perplexing problem. If God is a God of moral justice, how can He allow wicked men to prosper in their wickedness? Why doesn't He judge them? Why do they seem to "get away with it"?

Why do pornographers make millions? Why do presidents lie under oath and see their poll numbers go up? Why do deadbeat dads flee from their responsibilities while single moms toil to pay the bills? Why do murderers get off the hook and end up signing book deals instead of going to prison? On and on the list goes.

Asaph had pondered these questions deeply, and the

answers he received troubled him. In fact, his foothold in faith had almost slipped as he envied the arrogance of the wicked (vv. 2–3).

Arrogance is part of the conundrum. It's not just that the wicked prosper. That much we might be able to swallow. But it's their swaggering unconcern for anyone else, their bragging to their friends that crime really does pay. Either they think God doesn't know or God doesn't care, or maybe God is on their side (v. 11). O Lord, why do you allow such men to prosper? Why don't you strike them dead?

Worst of all, it makes the righteous feel we have kept our hands pure in vain. Why bother keeping the rules if the bad guys win by breaking the rules? Where is the reward for doing right?

The answer came in a strange way. Asaph went to the sanctuary of God to pray and to worship. There he encountered the God who stands above the teeming ways of humanity. There he learned again that "though the wheels of God grind slowly, they grind exceeding small."

In the words of Martin Luther King Jr., "The moral arc of the universe is long, but it bends toward justice."

Justice! That's the answer. *The wicked prosper in this life because they are about to suffer for all eternity*. They will soon be swept away by terrors they cannot begin to imagine (v. 19).

Are you tempted to doubt God's plan? Do you sometimes wonder if the wrong team will win in the end? Do not despair.

Go back to God's house, enter His sanctuary, dwell with His people, and let worship lead you to the truth. Those who serve God in this life will never regret it in the life to come. It's a grand thing to be a Christian when you die. If you know Jesus, the best is yet to come.

Do you envy those who are wicked? How foolish, how shortsighted. Let them have their short moment in the sun. For the wicked, this earth is the only heaven they will ever know. For the righteous, this earth is the only hell we will ever endure. Those who serve God in this life will never regret it in the life to come.

O God, I see many things that confuse me and many things that make no sense at all. Forgive me when I doubt Your wisdom. Restore my confidence in Your eternal plan. Amen.

1. Name three ways you see the wicked prospering.
2. Why doesn't God judge them right now?
3. What does it mean to you to "go to the sanctuary" of God?

TAKING GOD'S NAME IN VAIN

Remember how the enemy has mocked you, O Lord, how foolish people have reviled your name.

PSALM 74:18

Can you recite the third commandment?

The third commandment warns us not to take the Lord's name "in vain" (Exod. 20:7). But what does that mean?

God is not a toy you can play with casually and then put back on the shelf. It's like those warning signs that say, "Danger! High Voltage!" If you ignore the sign, you will soon be electrocuted. Psalm 74:18 reminds us God takes note of how His name is used—both by His friends and by His enemies. The foolish people who have reviled His name will soon learn that "God is a live wire" and His name is not to be taken lightly.

If that sounds strange, consider the story of Uzzah in 2 Samuel 6. King David had ordered the Ark of God be transported from Abinadab's house into Jerusalem. David's men put the Ark of God—"which is called by the Name"—on a cart, which was their first mistake. God had ordered the Levites should carry the Ark by inserting long poles through rings on the sides.

Perhaps they were in a hurry and thought it didn't matter. Two sons of Abinadab—Ahio and Uzzah—walked beside the cart to guide it and to protect it. As they approached the threshing floor of Nacon, the oxen stumbled, causing the Ark to sway on the cart. Uzzah immediately reached out his hand to steady the Ark. It was the last act of his life.

When he touched the Ark, God struck him dead. "The Lord's anger burned against Uzzah because of his irreverent act; therefore God struck him down, and he died there beside the ark of God" (2 Sam. 6:7).

That may seem like a huge overreaction to you. After all, Uzzah was only trying to do his job. But God was sending a message that no one should dare to trifle with His name. *Enthusiasm must be accompanied by obedience.*

Take God lightly ... and you will die! That's the message of Uzzah.

Are you surprised? Don't be. Don't great celebrities pay millions to protect their names? Don't major corporations hire hundreds of attorneys to ensure their corporate names are not misused? If you misuse a corporate symbol, you'll soon find yourself on the wrong end of a lawsuit.

God's name is important to Him. Misuse it, and He'll see you in court!

Sovereign Lord, You have warned me
of the dangers of irreverence. Help me
to take these words to heart. Amen.

1. Why is God's name so important to Him?
2. List several ways people misuse God's name.
3. What does the story of Uzzah tell us today?

WANTED: A GOOD MEMORY

I will remember the deeds of the Lord;
yes, I will remember your miracles of long ago.

PSALM 77:11

It's normal to forget the hard times.
Who wants to look back on yesterday's struggles?

Did God bring you through the wilderness this year? Don't forget what He did. Did God provide manna and quail to keep you alive? Don't forget His provision. Did God lead you with a cloud and a fiery pillar? Don't forget His guidance.

Moses told his people never to forget what God had done for them. He knew that when the Jews finally settled down in the Promised Land, it would be easy to forget the forty years in the wilderness. Moses understood that prosperity brings its own challenges. Bill Gates said it this way: "Success is a lousy teacher. It makes smart people think they can't lose."

That's the problem with winning. Once you think you can't lose, you feel invincible. At that point, you're about to become a loser. You just don't know it yet. You can win too much, too soon, too quickly. Before long, you prove the adage that it's a short step from victory to defeat. For all the problems that losing brings, at least it cures the illusion of invincibility.

Psalm 103:2 calls us to "Praise the Lord, O my soul, and

forget not all His benefits." That's important because most of us are better at complaining than praising. Sometimes we need to give ourselves a good talking-to. We're good at telling the Lord what we want Him to do for us. We need a good dose of Psalm 103 to wash out that complaining spirit and replace it with a heart of gratitude to the Lord.

- We must *think* before we can *thank*.
- We must *ponder* before we can *praise*.
- We must *remember* before we can *rejoice*.

A good memory of the right things can save us when trouble comes.

Has God blessed you? Write it down. Think often about it. Tell it to your children, your family, your friends. Pass it along so that future generations can tell the story after you are gone.

- Remember the Lord.
- Remember His goodness.
- Remember His faithfulness.

Let's focus on what God has already done for us. What specific prayers were answered? Can you remember desperate moments when God came through for you? Do you recall great fear that turned into great rejoicing? Did He help your loved ones when all hope was gone? Have you seen Him part the Red Sea for you? Did He destroy a few kings on your behalf? Recalling those moments deepens your faith in God and gives you confidence to face the future without fear.

Take time to remember the Lord today.

O Lord, when I count my blessings, I quickly run out of fingers, but I never run out of blessings from above. I pray for a good memory of the good things You have done for me. Amen.

1. What has God done for you?
2. Make a list of five things the Lord has done for you or your family in the last twelve months.
3. Spend time in prayer thanking Him for His goodness to you.

IMPOSSIBLE, DIFFICULT, DONE

He divided the sea and led them through;
he made the water stand firm like a wall.
PSALM 78:13

"There are three stages in any great work attempted for God: impossible, difficult, done." - Hudson Taylor

When God wants to do something big, He starts with something very small. When He wants to do the miraculous, He starts with the impossible. After all, when He sent His Son to the world, He didn't send Him to New York or Chicago or even to Rome. He sent Him to a little village called Bethlehem.

God loves to start small, because then He can show His power in a mighty way. He is also the only one who gets credit because most of us don't want credit for small beginnings. We'd rather start big and go from there. And we expect things to move rather quickly.

It's not hard to see why we think that way. After all, our motives are lifted to a higher plane when we do something for the Lord. We pray for God's guidance, we search the Scriptures for guidance, and we believe God is honored with our efforts.

And still, things move slowly. What we hope to finish

in days takes months. Soon, a year passes, and then another year, and it seems as if our wheels are stuck in mud. Faith lags, enthusiasm wanes, the curious become skeptical, and nagging, ragged doubts take dead aim at our confidence. One thing we quickly learn: It won't be as easy as we thought. And the fact that we are doing it for the Lord seems to make no difference at all.

Why should it be so? Couldn't the Lord have set this up another way? The answer, of course, is that He could—and sometimes He does. But mostly God lets us struggle and sweat and continue to trust in Him.

In the end we come at last to the Red Sea. The Egyptian army is moving in from the rear. To the left and right is the desert. And up ahead the impassable sea. This is life for all of us. The bad news is, there is no natural way through the Red Sea. The good news is, God loves to start with impossibility.

Whenever we start out to do something great or important or truly worthwhile, in the beginning it always seems impossible. And the more worthwhile it is, the more impossible it will seem. Cheer up! When we work for God, what starts out impossible soon becomes difficult and eventually is done.

Loving Lord, my life seems filled with impossibilities. Give me the courage to step forward by faith, trusting You for the miracles I need. Amen.

1. Name several biblical examples where God used something small (or something very unlikely) to accomplish something great.
2. If you could ask God to do one thing for you that seems impossible right now, what would it be?
3. Where have you seen the "impossible, difficult, done" cycle in your own experience?

CAN GOD SET A TABLE IN THE WILDERNESS?

They spoke against God, saying,
"Can God spread a table in the desert?"
PSALM 78:19

Can God spread a table in the desert?

No, He can't. God can't set a table in the desert. That's a foolish question because the wilderness is where you go to die. So the answer is no, God can't set a table in the wilderness. Or if He can, He won't. So, what's the difference? Thus said God's people, speaking against God. This is what happens whenever you forget what God has done.

The doubts were understandable. *It is a fearful thing in life to be "between trapezes."* That's a metaphor I learned a few years ago to describe the frightening moment when you leave the familiar for the unfamiliar.

The wilderness is not an easy place to be. It can seem …

- Dangerous,
- Lonely,
- Deadly,
- Risky,
- Hopeless.

It's easy to get lost there. You may spend a long time there. But it is also the place where you learn your own limitations, face your own failures, wrestle with temptation, learn to lean on others, find strength you didn't know you had, and see God work in unusual ways.

Where (or what) is your wilderness?

- An unpleasant person?
- A difficult work situation?
- Learning to deal with grief?
- Losing your job?
- Your own boring life?
- Fear that grips your heart?
- Cancer that grows inside you?
- A father who abandoned you?
- A sick child?
- Paralyzing depression?
- The church where you pastor?
- The town you hate?
- The family you would rather not see?
- A marriage slowly dying?

Can God prepare a table in a place like that? Can God meet you right where you are? Can God spread a table amid your personal wilderness?

Can God set a table in the wilderness? Yes, He can. But you'll never know as long as you stay in Egypt. By definition, you have to be in the wilderness first. Only then can God set a table for you. *God never leads us into the wilderness in order to destroy us.* He intends the time of testing to make us stronger.

It's far better to be in the wilderness with Jesus than

in a fancy penthouse without Him. Life isn't about your dreams, agenda, hopes, ideas, or plans. Life is all about God's dreams, God's agenda, God's ideas, and God's plans. It's His kingdom we're praying to come, not ours.

Can God set a table in the wilderness? He can. He does. He will. You can count on it. Let all God's people say, amen.

Lord God, teach me to trust You while I trek through the wilderness. Thank You for providing for me even when I doubt that You will. Amen.

1. What wilderness have you walked through recently?
2. How did God "set a table" for you?
3. Why are we so quick to forget what God has done for us?

YOU CAN'T ARGUE PEOPLE INTO THE KINGDOM

In spite of all this, they kept on sinning;
in spite of his wonders, they did not believe.

PSALM 78:32

Some people never learn.

Even after all the miracles, God's people never seemed to learn to serve God. That's the point of Psalm 78. Here God's people are wandering in the wilderness, guided by the cloud and the fire, fed with manna and quail, yet they constantly complain against the Lord. In other words, they were just like us!

That's why you can't argue people into the kingdom. It just doesn't work. You can quote Scripture by the yard, make every apologetic argument, convince them they are sinners and Jesus is a wonderful Savior, but until the Spirit moves, they will not respond.

Earlier generations talked about "soul winning," an admirable term for sharing Christ with the lost. But we are not the real "soul winners." That role belongs only to the Holy Spirit. We witness, but only the Holy Spirit can draw sinners to Jesus.

"A man convinced against his will is of the same opinion still." That's why you can quote Spurgeon or Calvin or

Billy Graham. You can talk about Francis Schaeffer or Billy Sunday, but it won't matter. You can use clever illustrations and even share your own story. Without the Holy Spirit, it won't change a single heart.

Sometimes I run into people who will not believe no matter what I say to them. It's almost like there's a barrier between me and them. As a matter of fact, there is a barrier between me and them, which is why it is impossible to argue anybody into the kingdom of God. You cannot do it.

Evangelism is more than imparting information. We share the Good News of Jesus in the most winsome way possible, but only the Holy Spirit can change the human heart.

Some people don't believe because they don't want to believe, and nothing you can say can convince them otherwise. We may wonder why unbelievers won't respond to our arguments. Even after we answer all their questions and fully explain the gospel, why won't they come to Christ? It's because their questions weren't the real problem. The questions were a smoke screen to cover up a hardened heart.

Only the Holy Spirit can convict men and women of their sin before God (John 16:8–11). That isn't easy to do. It's easy to get people to admit they're not perfect. Almost everybody will admit that. People will admit they've done wrong from time to time. They will gladly agree to the occasional mistake.

But it is difficult to get men and women to admit they are sinners before a holy God. In fact, it is so difficult, it is humanly impossible. That's why you can't argue a person into the kingdom. The next time you tell others about Christ, be bold, be gracious, and keep smiling.

Let the Holy Spirit do the rest.

Spirit of God, give me holy boldness and
a winsome spirit as I talk about
Christ with others. Amen.

1. Have you ever had an experience similar to the one described above?
2. How can we convince sinners of their need for a Savior?
3. What usually happens when we try to argue people into God's kingdom?

DANGEROUS TEMPTATIONS

But my people would not listen
to me; Israel would not submit to me.
So I gave them over to their stubborn
hearts to follow their own devices.

PSALM 81:11–12

Here is a solemn word from the Lord.

If we fight against God, He will eventually give us over to our own desires. If we insist on going our own way, in the end God will grant our request—often to our own eternal regret.

A woman sat in my office and told me the saddest story I have heard in many years. She was raised as a Christian and at one time had a strong faith in Jesus Christ. But during a period of loneliness, she fell in with a bad crowd and began to dabble in sin, a little here and a little there.

Eventually she began to experiment with drugs. She became hooked on heroin, so much so that she resorted to terrible extremes to finance her drug habit. But when she gets high, she starts to talk about God. We quoted Bible verses together in my office.

At one point I told her if she didn't make the decision to come clean, it wouldn't be long before I spoke at her funeral. Then I challenged her to become a woman of truth because the truth would set her free. My parting words were the words of Jesus, "Go now and leave your life of sin" (John 8:11). She smiled and thanked me and said she needed to go and get some heroin, or she wouldn't make it through the day. Then she walked out of my office.

Fast forward 25 years. When I saw her recently, the change in her was remarkable. God answered many prayers and broke her addiction to heroin. She is free and clean and so happy. In fact, she now joyfully serves the Lord in her local church.

Her story illustrates both sides of this truth. When the Lord turned her over to her base desires, her addictions almost killed her. But when she finally turned to the Lord, and with the help of wise friends who prayed for her, God's mighty power gave her a new life. It was not instant or easy. There were tears and doubt and a hard battle to fight. But the Lord broke the power of those "dangerous temptations."

What happened to her can happen to any of us if we respond wrongly to hard times. Let no one condemn her but instead let us consider our own lives and realize how vulnerable we are to Satan's attacks.

And let's rejoice that Jesus is still in the life-changing business. He knows how to set the prisoner free.

Lord, when I am tempted to look down on others, help me to remember that "there but for the grace of God go I." May I never take Your protection for granted. Amen.

1. Can you think of a time when you wished for something—only to regret it later?
2. Where are you currently vulnerable to Satan's attacks?
3. Where do you feel you are strong, and thus you might be vulnerable to Satan's attacks?

AFTER DEATH, WHAT THEN?

But you will die like mere men;
you will fall like every other ruler.
PSALM 82:7

When you cross the line,
there is no coming back from the other side.

How can we explain the universal fascination with the world beyond the grave? Is it not because death is so final? Whatever one thinks about the reports of "near-death" visions, death when it finally comes is irreversible.

Death wins the battle every time. After the doctors have tried the latest wonder drug, after the best minds have pooled their wisdom, after the philosophers have done their best to explain that death is only a natural part of life, we come face-to-face with the ugly reality that someday we will all die. And that death—whether expected or accidental, whether comfortable or painful—will be the end of life as we have known it.

No wonder the human mind is drawn to the question, "What happens when we die?" In many ways it is the one remaining unanswered question. We know so much about so many things, but about life after death, we know so very little.

Every person must answer three great questions:

- Where did I come from?
- Why am I here?
- Where am I going?

It is the third question that most grips the heart of man, for in one sense, the question "Where did I come from?" is yesterday's news, and the question "Why am I here?" is one we answer every day, but the third question takes us into the unseen future—into the unfolding years and decades.

What happens when we die? Is death the end of everything? Does man live for a few years and then simply vanish from the screen? Do we simply play our part and then shuffle off the stage into the misty obscurity of nothingness? Or is there something more, something beyond the great divide?

Thousands of years ago, Job spoke for the rest of us when he asked, "If a man dies, will he live again?" (Job 14:14). In answering questions about life after death, we are left with only two sources to consult. Either we turn to human experience, or we turn to the Word of God.

If we turn to human experience, we find many guesses, many ideas, many theories—but no sure answers. That's because, in the nature of the case, no human has a sure answer. The only people who have the answer are dead. That leaves us with the Word of God. In the Bible we find abundant answers. The God who knows the future also knows what happens when we die, and He hasn't left us to wonder about it.

Let's revisit Job's question for a moment: "If a man dies, will he live again?" (Job 14:14). The answer is yes. If you know Jesus, you live forever with Him. The child of God need not fear death for the grave has lost its victory. In the hour of death if you know Jesus you may be sure the grave is but a doorway to glory.

Lord, since I will live forever somewhere,
I pray to be prepared to spend
eternity with You. Amen.

1. Picture the moment of your own death. How do you expect it will happen?
2. Do you fear that moment?
3. Describe what you think will happen to you the first five minutes after your death.

SLOW DOWN!

My soul yearns, even faints, for the courts of the Lord; my heart and my flesh cry out for the living God.

PSALM 84:2

Why can't we experience God's presence every day?

This week I had a chance to stop and worship God in an extended way for the first time in seven years. I spent four days with seventy-five other pastors in a Pastor's Prayer Summit.

In my years as a pastor, I've been to many camps, conferences, and retreats, but never have I been to anything like a Prayer Summit. For four days—from Monday afternoon until Thursday noon—we met with no agenda but worshiping God.

There were no sermons, no bulletins, and no set program. We simply gathered in a large circle and waited for God to speak to us. Sometimes we sang together, sometimes we bowed in silent prayer, often we prayed together.

On Tuesday, the leaders put a chair in the middle of the circle and offered pastors a chance to ask for prayer for their personal needs. I saw pastors weeping over their sins and grown men embracing each other with words of healing and forgiveness.

It was an awesome experience for me personally. But as I look back, I realize I was so wound up when I got there that it took me two days to relax enough to enjoy it. And about the time I started getting in the swing of things, it was time to go home.

On our last night there, someone spontaneously prayed, "Lord, wouldn't it be great if what happened here could happen every day to every man when we go back home." It would be great, wouldn't it?

Why can't we experience God's presence every day? Whatever answer you give to that question, just remember God is not the problem. He's always ready to meet you any time of the day or night.

Does your heart cry out for the living God? Do you yearn for the courts of the Lord? Or have the demands of a busy schedule and the reality of overcommitment stifled your desire for the Lord?

As with so many other areas of life, the problem is within us. *We're too busy to hear God's voice.* We're running so hard and so fast God would have to shout to get our attention. Sometimes that's what He does. He shouts through pain or opposition or sickness or disappointment, and suddenly we begin to hear His voice.

It doesn't have to be that way. God always speaks loud enough for a listening ear to hear.

Slow me down, Lord, so I can hear
Your still, small voice again. Amen.

1. How long has it been since you slowed down for more than a few minutes?
2. What happens to people who run in "high gear" all the time?
3. How can you alter your schedule to include more time to listen to God's voice?

ABOUNDING IN FAITHFULNESS

But you, O Lord, are a
compassionate and gracious God,
slow to anger, abounding in
love and faithfulness.
PSALM 86:15

Think about the word *abounding* for a moment.

To abound in money means to have all the money you need—and plenty more besides. To abound in land means your ranch is so big it stretches beyond the horizon. To abound in faithfulness means no one will ever reach the end of it.

This truth should give us enormous confidence in God. If you have doubted God, doubt no longer. He is faithful to keep His promises. He has ordained that someday you will be like the Lord Jesus inside and out. And He is working even now to make you a better person. Even though you can't always see His hand at work, don't doubt His purposes.

God's faithfulness is the ground of our assurance. Sometimes believers struggle with assurance because we don't "feel" saved. But feelings have nothing to do with it. If you feel saved, that's good, and you should be grateful. But if you don't feel saved, trust God to keep His word anyway.

Salvation rests not on your fickle feelings but on the unchanging promises of a God who cannot lie.

Since God is faithful, we have the ultimate motivation for spiritual growth. After all, if God has said He will sanctify you, you can rest assured you will be sanctified—even if right now you would rather stay as you are. Your only choice is whether or not you will cooperate with God. Some of us get better slower than necessary because we fight against God's purposes.

We harbor wrong attitudes—lust, bitterness, pride, sloth, envy, and all the rest—and then we wonder why it's taking us so long to get better. A little cooperation goes a long way in the area of sanctification.

Finally, God's faithfulness ought to give us perseverance in prayer. Sometimes we stop praying two days before the answer comes from heaven. I know many Christians who have struggled for years with certain behavior patterns and then given up simply because they were so discouraged.

But the Bible tells us God is always at work, moving us toward a time when we will be perfect in every respect. Even in this life, we can make huge progress as Christians. It's just that progress often comes slowly and in small increments.

We keep praying precisely because we believe God is at work in us even when we don't see it.

Lord, I do not pray for more faith.
I ask instead for a greater understanding
of Your faithfulness. Amen.

1. How would you respond to a believer who says he doesn't "feel" saved?
2. In what way is God's faithfulness the basis for our assurance?
3. What kind of "cooperation" have you given God lately?

WE'RE MARCHING TO ZION

The L*ORD* *loves the gates of Zion*
more than all the dwellings of Jacob.
PSALM 87:2

Jesus introduces us to the throne room of the universe.

Originally Mount Zion was the name of the hill on which the city of Jerusalem was built. Later, Zion became the name of Jerusalem itself. Whenever Zion is mentioned, it is the earthly dwelling place of God. In the Old Testament, the Jews would come marching to Zion, the city of Jerusalem, where they would meet their God.

By the time of the New Testament, Zion came to represent heaven, God's eternal dwelling place. Everything we think of when we think about heaven is part of what the New Testament calls Zion. As in the Old Testament, there was a physical Zion and a physical city called Jerusalem, so in the New Testament, there is a spiritual Mount Zion and a heavenly Jerusalem.

Hebrews 12:22 says, "But you have come to Mount Zion." The word the author used for *come* means to draw near, to come alongside. *As Christians we have drawn near to heaven.* In Jesus Christ we have come near to ultimate spiritual reality.

There is more to the universe than meets the eye. The realm of spiritual reality cannot be measured in a test tube.

Did you know there are thousands of voices all around you? Maybe tens of thousands. Where are they? Why can't you hear them? The voices are on radio waves from all over the world talking in dozens of languages. Add to that television signals, microwave phone signals, and satellite transmissions surrounding you on every side. We cannot see them or hear them because we aren't tuned in to the right frequency. But no one doubts they are there.

In Jesus Christ, we have come near to God and to heaven and to heavenly reality. Jesus introduces us to the throne room of the universe. Every time we pray, we come near to God. Every time we worship together, heaven is not far away. We draw near to the angels every time we sing a Christian song.

We are in God's presence, surrounded by angels, enrolled in heaven, accepted by God, not far from our loved ones, forgiven by the blood. We have something wonderful in Jesus. We live next door to heaven.

When we are tempted to go back to the old life, we remember we have something infinitely greater at our disposal—God and Jesus and the church and the angels and our loved ones and Mount Zion and heaven itself.

We have come to Mount Zion, and we intend to stay there. Nothing could improve our position. We're not going back, because the world has nothing better to offer.

Heavenly Father, Your blessings are so great that all the gold and silver in the world is nothing compared to the things You have prepared for us. Help me to live as one made rich by Your grace. Amen.

1. Take a piece of paper and jot down at least seven blessings that are yours through Jesus Christ.
2. What does it mean to you that "heaven is not far away"?
3. Do you agree the world has nothing better to offer?

YOU WON'T LIVE FOREVER

Teach us to number our days aright,
that we may gain a heart of wisdom.
PSALM 90:12

Dust in the wind. That's all we are.

One hymn says it this way: "Frail children of dust, and feeble as frail." We are here today and gone tomorrow—" like the new grass of the morning" that springs up fresh and by evening it is dry and withered (vv. 5–6).

Ashes to ashes, and dust to dust. If we are all dust in the wind, how can we find meaning in life? I heard a well-known public figure say we're all like pop bottles on a conveyor belt. We drop on the belt, ride a little way, and then we fall off the belt, only to be replaced by another bottle.

Not a very uplifting view of life, is it? But it is partly true. From one perspective we show up at birth, grow up, get old, and then we die, apparently to be replaced by someone younger. Where is the dignity in that?

Psalm 90:4 adds a crucial fact to the mix: "For a thousand years in your sight are like a day that has just gone by, or like a watch in the night." God stands above history. He and He alone provides a meaningful context for the few years we live on planet Earth. What seems so important to us is nothing in eternity's grand scheme. In his great hymn "Immortal, Invisible," Walter Chalmers Smith wrote this verse:

To all life Thou givest, to both great and small;
In all life Thou livest, the true life of all;
We blossom and flourish, like leaves on the tree,
They wither and perish, but naught changeth Thee.

God's perspective is radically different from ours. He works across the centuries to accomplish His purposes. There is no reason to boast when we could wither away at any moment.

As our family gathered for a meal late one December my wife said, "Let's thank God for all His blessings during this year." Our youngest son immediately spoke up and said, "The year's not over yet. One of us could die today."

True, and that's exactly the point Moses was making.

Lest this seem morbid, remember that a healthy sense of your own mortality can help you make wise decisions. That's why we need to "number our days."

Recently I tried to calculate how much longer I was going to live. As of this moment, I've lived 26,126 days. I'm 71 going on what? 75? 80? 85? Who knows? I may be gone before you read these words—or I may live twenty more years. But I won't be here forever, so I'd best number my days and use each one to serve God while I can.

Lord, teach me to number my days
so that I might use them for Your glory.
Help me to remember that I won't
be here forever. Amen.

1. Take a moment to calculate the number of days you have lived so far.
2. Now, guess how many more days you expect to live.
3. What is the most eternally profitable way you can spend your remaining days?

UNDER HIS WINGS

A thousand may fall at your side,
ten thousand at your right hand,
but it will not come near you.

PSALM 91:7

This verse has sustained many a believer in the heat of battle.

How can a captain lead his troops into the teeth of withering enemy fire? Is it not because he believes so fervently in his cause that he considers himself invincible to enemy bullets?

By the same token, this verse encourages us to believe that when we face opposition on every side, we can enter the fray knowing nothing can harm us unless God wills it. Sometimes we are spared altogether, sometimes we are wounded that we might trust even more in our God, and sometimes we are hit but not hurt.

This verse teaches us that we may have extraordinary courage in the moment of great crisis. We can stand when others fall around us. We can face our problems boldly. We can go into surgery with confidence, we can be dragged into court, we can be called on the carpet at work, we can face dangers as we travel.

We can do all that because we know the Lord is with us. Does this mean nothing bad can happen to the child of God? No, because bad things happen to God's people all the time. Romans 8:28 tells us "All things work together for good to them that love God" (KJV), yet just a few verses later Paul spoke of peril, nakedness, the sword, persecution and famine (vv. 35–36). All these things—and more—happen to Christians.

What is Psalm 91 telling us?

- God's care extends to the tiniest details of life.
- Nothing bad happens to us by chance.
- God is able to deliver us in the worst circumstances.

Nothing can touch the child of God that has not first passed through His hands of love. Does that include the worst? Yes, it does. Nothing can hurt us without God's permission. Not the enemy, not financial ruin, not divorce, not lies and slander, not cancer, not strange accidents. Not disrespectful children. Not an unfaithful husband. Not a sudden loss of a job. Not scandal, rumor, or innuendo. Not an unfair lawsuit. Not a failed insurance policy. Not even death itself. Not Satan and his tricks. Not the fiery darts of the devil. Not the demons of hell. None of it can touch us except by God's permission.

Most of the time we won't understand when arrows hit us. But in our confusion, our despair, our uncertainty, when we don't know anything else, we know this much: *God has planned it all for our good and His glory.* For the children of God, there are no accidents—only incidents.

The hymn writer said it well:

When all around my soul gives way,
He then is all my hope and stay.

On Christ, the solid Rock, I stand;
All other ground is sinking sand,
All other ground is sinking sand.

Lord, You are the solid rock of my life. Give me firm footing so that I will not slide off. Amen.

1. Do you agree nothing bad can happen to you without God's permission?
2. How does that truth affect the way you view your problems?
3. Name an "accident" that became an "incident" that God used in a positive way in your life.

A ONE-WORD PRAYER

He will call upon me, and I will answer him;
I will be with him in trouble, I will
deliver him and honor him.

PSALM 91:15

What is the simplest prayer of all? Help!

When you don't know what else to pray, that will usually do just fine.

Psalm 91:14–16 shows us God's eight-fold deliverance of His people:

1. I will rescue him.
2. I will protect him.
3. I will answer him.
4. I will be with him.
5. I will deliver him.
6. I will honor him.
7. I will satisfy him.
8. I will save him.

There is a progression here. *First*, God meets us where we are. He finds us in the moment of our deep need. *Second*, He promises to be with us no matter what we are going through. *Third*, He will deliver us—sooner or later, one way or the other. *Fourth*, He promises to bestow glory and honor upon us. *Fifth*, He satisfies us with a full life—not long years necessarily, but fullness of life no matter how many years we mark on the calendar. *Sixth*, He will one day show us the full extent of His salvation when we see Jesus in heaven.

God draws a line from the difficulties of this life and says, "Follow Me and I will lead you straight to heaven." We think our problems are so large. God says, "Don't sweat the small stuff. I'm going to take you to heaven someday. I can handle your problems."

This week I read about a woman who said, "Before I go to bed, I give all my problems to the Lord. He's going to be up all night anyway." Indeed, He is.

Not long ago I began taking inventory of my problems—and felt greatly discouraged. All of them are bigger than I am. All are beyond my puny strength to solve by myself. As I pondered the matter, one insight seemed to help: God has promised to be with me. He has invited me to call upon Him for all my needs. He has said He would be with me in the time of trouble and would at the right moment deliver me. *Even Satan himself cannot harm me without God's divine permission.*

With that confidence, I go on.

I like the way Eugene Peterson paraphrased verse 14: "'If you'll hold on to me for dear life,' says God, 'I'll get you out of any trouble'" (MSG). You don't have to deliver yourself. You don't even have to try. All you have to do is hold on for dear life. God Himself will do the rest.

Whatever your problem, whatever your difficulty, whatever things keep you awake at night, hold on for dear life. Help is on the way.

Father, I rest in the confidence that I will be delivered from all my difficulties sooner or later. Grant that it might be sooner. Amen.

1. Take an inventory of your problems, worries, and current concerns.
2. Which ones can you handle and which ones obviously need divine intervention?
3. Spend some time committing each one to the Lord.

WORRY: THE FRUIT OF A DIVIDED MIND

When anxiety was great
within me, your consolation
brought joy to my soul.

PSALM 94:19

Our problems are, at heart, theological.

The word *anxiety* comes from a root that means "to divide." That's because anxiety produces a divided mind, one which is pulled this way and that way, constantly distracted and disturbed.

Here's the point: Either the Lord carries the worry, or we do. If we do, we'll be divided, distracted, and disturbed. And we will end up confused, frustrated, and burdened. If He carries the load, we may still have trouble and difficulties, but no anxiety, no dominating fear, no undue concern, no hopeless despair.

There's a reason we can do that with confidence— "your consolation brought joy to my soul." This touches a secret fear of many believers—*that if we submit our lives to Jesus Christ, He'll mess things up. He'll ask us to do things we don't want to do; He'll send us places we don't want to go; He'll bring unpleasant people into our lives and force us to be someone we don't want to be.* And we secretly fear He can't be trusted to take care of us. So, we decide to live at a 60 or 70 percent level of trust and wonder why we are so bored, frustrated, and unfulfilled spiritually.

Our problems are at heart theological. We've never settled the question, what kind of God do we believe in? In biblical terms, we've never settled the question of whether we believe God really cares for us. We think He does; we hope He does, but many days we're not sure.

When you get right down to it, we're not sure about God: We can't quite bring ourselves to trust Him. Until we, by a conscious choice, settle the big question, "What kind of God do I believe in?" all lesser questions will go unanswered.

Here is the genius of biblical Christianity: God cares for me. And He proved it by sending His own Son to die for me. At the Cross the issue was settled for eternity. Any God who would sacrifice His own Son for a person like me must care for me. There's no other reason He would do such a thing.

When we come to God, we don't have to convince Him to hear us. We don't have to chant or shout or burn incense or ring bells or use a priest or offer a sacrifice. No, we come as His children, and He gladly hears us. We don't do anything to make God care.

We begin and act from the assurance, rooted in history, that God cares for us. On that basis we can unload all our worries on Him.

Lord Jesus, help me to discern the difference between honest concern and sinful worry. Show me how to cast my cares upon You lest I collapse under the weight of my own problems. Amen.

1. What are your top five worries/burdens/concerns right now?
2. Who is better able to handle those things—you or God?
3. If the answer is God, take time right now to roll your burdens on the Lord. If the answer is you, go back and read this entry again.

IT'S TIME TO KNEEL BEFORE THE LORD

Come, let us bow down in worship,
let us kneel before the Lord *our Maker.*

PSALM 95:6

Are you ready to kneel before the Lord?

Before you answer, consider this. The wise men weren't ashamed to kneel down. Matthew 2:11 says when they saw Jesus with His mother, they bowed down and worshiped Him. When the wise men finally found the baby Jesus, were they disappointed? They might have been. After such a long journey and after the detour in Jerusalem, did it seem anticlimactic?

It might have seemed that way: He did not look like a king. His home did not look like a castle. He had no scepter in His hand, commanded no armies, gave no speeches, passed no laws. No royal decree came from His lips.

There was nothing to make you think He was a king. To the outward eye, He was nothing but a peasant child born in dire poverty. But to the wise men, He was a king. He possessed more royalty in a cradle than Herod possessed in his fine palace. He was greater in His infancy than Louis XIV in his ascendancy. He was more powerful as a child than Napoleon as an emperor.

But it did not seem that way. The eyes of flesh revealed nothing but a normal baby, gurgling and cooing, moving His tiny hands side to side, reaching eagerly for His mother's breast. The wise men saw beyond the present, and in deep faith they worshiped Him. They saw that this child would one day rule the world, and they were not ashamed to fall on their faces before Him.

Let me paraphrase the words of one Bible commentator: Although we read that the wise men met Herod, we do not read that they worshiped him. But when they found this tiny baby, these great men fell on their faces before Him. To this baby they gave the honor due to a king. What Herod craved, the baby received.

Kneeling does not come easy for most of us. We stand or we sit, but we rarely kneel. Kneeling requires us to admit we are in the presence of someone greater than us. There is no kneeling among equals.

The wise men offer a lesson to us today. These great men, highly respected and well-educated, having traveled so far, understood who Jesus was. God's Spirit had led them from somewhere in the east (Persia, perhaps) to a distant land, among people they did not know, to a house in the tiny village of Bethlehem.

No doubt others knelt before them in their homeland. But they do not hesitate to bow before Jesus because they understand what royalty demands.

Lord Jesus, we kneel in Your presence because
You are greater than we can imagine.
Be glorified in my life today. Amen.

1. Under what circumstances would you bow before another person?
2. Have you ever bowed in worship before the Lord?
3. Why is the physical act of bowing (or kneeling) important in our worship?

THE OIL OF THE SPIRITUAL LIFE

Worship the Lord *in the splendor of his holiness;*
tremble before him, all the earth.

PSALM 96:9

If your God is holy, you will become holy.

My favorite definition of worship comes from William Temple, Archbishop of Canterbury many years ago:

> To worship is to quicken the conscience by the holiness of God, to feed the mind with the truth of God, to purge the imagination with the beauty of God, to open the heart to the love of God, to devote the will to the purpose of God.

Worship is the central point of the Christian life, and when we make it first, everything else falls into place.

One fine spring morning in Texas, I noticed the sun was coming out, the grass was beginning to grow, and it was time to bring out the lawn mower. When it wouldn't start, I kept pulling until I finally broke the rope. Then I checked the spark plug and put it back in place.

I put my fingers in the gas chamber and found dirty fuel from the past fall. I checked a few other connections and found everything in working order. The blades were sharp and ready to go—no problem there. I took it to a repair shop, where they said they would fix it.

A few days later it was ready. They'd had to replace something in the engine. I asked what the matter was. They said there was no oil in the motor. For some reason it had never occurred to me to put oil in a lawn mower. When the oil had run out, the motor wouldn't run anymore.

Behold this simple truth: *Worship is the oil of the spiritual life*. When you run low on worship, your life starts to break down. If you feel a little broken down, it may not be because you are busy, but because you have run low on worship.

Psalm 96 calls us to worship God "in the splendor of His holiness." Whether we like it or not, we become like what we worship. If your god is evil, you will become evil. If your god is greedy, you will become greedy. But if your God is holy, you will become holy.

Would you like to become beautiful? Then focus your mind and heart on the living God. His beauty will make you beautiful. You will become like Jesus!

It all comes down to this. If you ever get a glimpse of what Jesus has done for you, you'll never play church again. The hymn writer said it well:

What language shall I borrow
To thank thee, dearest Friend,
For this thy dying sorrow,
Thy pity without end?
O make me thine for ever;
And should I fainting be,
Lord, let me never, never
Outlive my love to thee.

When you lift the worship of God back to its proper place, your life will start working again.

Holy God, quicken my heart that I might worship You in spirit and in truth. Amen.

1. Are you "running low" on worship?
2. What do you need to do about it?
3. Take a moment to reread William Temple's definition of worship; which of those characteristics do you most need in your life right now?

COMING SOON

Let those who love the Lord hate evil,
for he guards the lives of his faithful ones and
delivers them from the hand of the wicked.

PSALM 97:10

Arthur Clarke gave Psalm 97 the title
"Coming in the Clouds."

The connection with the Second Coming of Christ seems apt since verses 1–6 call the earth to rejoice when His righteousness is finally revealed. Verse 7 warns of judgment to come on idolaters. Verses 8–9 declare that Israel will rejoice when the Lord, the Most High, reigns on the earth. The final three verses of this short psalm promise deliverance for the faithful and light for the righteous who are called upon to praise the name of the Lord.

The most striking fact about this psalm is that the writer (who is not named) used the past tense, yet he spoke of events future to him (and to us). That is, he wrote with such certainty about the Second Coming that it was as if it had already happened.

Someday soon the Lord will return to the earth. But how soon is soon? Nearly three thousand years have passed since Psalm 97 was written, and two thousand years have passed since Jesus walked on the earth. No wonder skeptics cry out, "Where is the promise of His coming?"

(2 Pet. 3:4 KJV). Yet they forget a day with the Lord is like a thousand years and a thousand years is like a day.

The people who scoffed at Noah later drowned when water covered the whole earth. No doubt they laughed about "nutty Noah" and his "crazy boat," but the door was closed when the rains came down and they had nowhere else to turn. In the days of Noah, unbelievers went merrily about their daily business. They were eating and drinking, marrying and giving in marriage until the very day when Noah entered the ark (Matt. 24:37–39). Suddenly they were swept away by the rising floodwaters.

Something similar will happen when Christ returns for His faithful people. They will be saved, but the wicked will be swept away. That day is coming—and we pray it will come soon. All signs point in that direction. But whether Christ comes today or tomorrow or not for a thousand years, God's promise is certain. Christ will return to the earth and will reign from David's throne in Jerusalem.

Let's stay faithful to the Lord no matter how long we have to wait. Christ will return, and the scoffers will be silenced forever.

Lord Jesus, more than anything else,
I want to hear You say, "Well done, good and
faithful servant." Help me to stay strong
when others mock my faith. Amen.

1. Why is faithfulness so important to God?
2. How does God reward faithfulness in this life?
3. How does He reward faithfulness in the life to come?

TO EVERY GENERATION

His faithfulness continues through all generations.

PSALM 100:5

God's faithfulness is contingent upon His unchanging character.

Consider the final phrase of Psalm 100: "through all generations." It literally means "from generation to generation." Exodus 20:6 tells us that God shows His love to "a thousand generations" of those who love Him. Since a biblical generation is 40 years, God's love lasts at least 40,000 years. And since this promise was given to Moses at Mt. Sinai approximately 3500 years ago, we may safely conclude God's faithful love will continue at least another 36,500 years. That is to say, in 3500 years we are not yet even 10% of the way through the length of God's love.

But surely that is not literal, you say. Indeed, it is not. But it is not purely figurative either. It's a way of showing us that God's love and faithfulness go far beyond any human understanding.

Suppose we line up a grandfather, a son, a grandson, and a great-grandson on the platform. This text tells us that what God was to the grandfather, He will be to the son. What He is to the son, He will be to the grandson. What He is to the grandson, He will be to the great-grandson. And so it goes across the centuries. Generations come and go, one after the other. Only God remains forever.

I am so glad God's faithfulness transcends the generations. I am 71 years old heading for … what? 75? 80? 85? Maybe even 90 years old if God blesses me with long life. But I won't live forever. As the years roll by, I find myself realizing how much of my life is wrapped up in my three sons. Yesterday they were teenagers, today they are fathers, the day after that they will be grandfathers.

Will God continue to care for our eleven grandchildren? Will He still be there for them? *The answer is a resounding yes. God's faithfulness is not contingent on my presence, but on His unchanging character that spans the generations.* This means I don't have to live forever to ensure the well-being of our children and grandchildren. God will take care of that.

Even after I depart from this earth, and even if all my prayers are not answered, I can rest assured that God will continue to care for my family. What a source of comfort this is. After I'm gone, God's faithfulness will persist for our children, our grandchildren, and even for the great-grandchildren who are yet to be born.

I do not know how much time we have left until we reach the end of our earthly road. But this I know: That road is paved with God's love and faithfulness. And we need not be afraid.

Because God is faithful, we can trust Him with the generations yet to come. Here is great hope for parents who worry about their children. *The God who cares for us will care for our children—and their children's children—too.*

Almighty God, Your faithfulness spans the generations. Thank You for being there for my children and grandchildren even after I'm gone from this earth. Amen.

1. How do you plan to pass your faith down to the next generation?
2. How does God's faithfulness give you confidence to live without fear?
3. Take a moment and thank God for His faithfulness to your great-great-grandchildren.

NO COMPROMISE!

Men of perverse heart shall be far from me;
I will have nothing to do with evil.

PSALM 101:4

We live in a world that no longer believes in truth.

I once heard that the world is in "the Age of Enlightenment Skepticism." That means we live in a world that no longer believes in truth. In another day, men and women argued passionately about the truth; today we argue whether truth even exists, and if it does, how can anyone know the truth? We are no longer sure as a culture how to determine right from wrong—or even if we should make the effort.

Many believe truth exists in the eye of the beholder—"That's true for you but not necessarily for me." Truth becomes an entirely private affair with no implications for society at large.

Against that growing trend we have these solemn words of David. They remind us that many false teachers are themselves the very spirit of untruth. These "men of perverse heart" deny the very concept of truth—and they travel from place to place peddling their spiritual poison. Christians must reject such teachers—to the point of refusing them any personal welcome. If we do welcome them, we are guilty of sharing in their evil deeds.

Strong words indeed—but greatly needed in this day of

immense spiritual confusion. Believers must aggressively oppose and refute false teaching and false teachers. To do less is to traffic with the enemies of the Cross and mock everything we believe.

These are exceedingly strong words, and one can wonder why David should feel impressed to write so bluntly. I know the answer. The longer we condone error, the easier it is to compromise. Little by little we become conditioned to moral decline and intellectual apostasy until it no longer seems so wrong to us.

- What we do not oppose, we tolerate.
- What we tolerate, we accept.
- What we accept, we praise.
- What we praise, we practice.

It may not happen overnight. In fact, the process of spiritual decline may take its course over the years, the decades, and the generations, but in the end the bills come due for not standing for the truth.

Most of us know the famous illustration about the frog in the kettle. Put a frog in a kettle with cold water and the frog will sit contentedly. Now slowly turn up the heat a few degrees at a time. Because the frog's system has time to adjust, he doesn't notice the changing temperature. When the water finally reaches a boil, the frog senses danger and tries to jump out, but it's too late. His legs won't move anymore.

Something like that happens to us when we coddle evil instead of facing it head-on and calling it what it is. When we refuse to oppose that which is wrong, evil doesn't look so bad.

Lord, make me so sensitive to You that I will be sensitive to sin. I want to love what You love and hate what You hate. Amen.

1. In what ways have you become "desensitized" to sin either in your own life or as it exists in society at large?
2. What steps do you need to take in this area?
3. Pray for discernment and for moral courage to do the right thing.

ANGELS EVERYWHERE!

Praise the Lord, *you his angels,*
you mighty ones who do his
bidding, who obey his word.
PSALM 103:20

Have you ever seen an angel?

For most of us, the answer is no. Angels are usually invisible. But now and then God pulls back the curtain and lets us see what is going on in heaven. That's what happened one night long ago in the fields around Bethlehem. Suddenly the angels showed up!

If we had been there, would we have seen them? Could the sound of their voices be heard in other places, or did the angels reveal themselves only to the shepherds? We cannot fully answer these questions, but this much is certain: The angels were really there, and the shepherds really did hear them.

Who are the angels? They are spirit beings who serve God in heaven. Evidently, they have many functions, including guarding the heavenly throne, praising God, doing battle with the demons, and protecting the people of God. Hebrews 1:14 calls them "ministering spirits" who are sent to serve the people of God.

Matthew 18:10 speaks of little children and "their angels," a reference to guardian angels in heaven who watch over the people of God. Daniel 10 speaks of a great struggle in the unseen realm between the angels and the demonic forces of the devil.

The dramatic story is told of Elisha and his servant at Dothan when they were surrounded by the armies of Aram. The servant was frightened until Elisha prayed that his eyes might be opened. Then he saw "the hills full of horses and chariots of fire all around Elisha" (2 Kings 6:17).

The angels are closer to us than we think. Hebrews 12:22 says that in Christ we have come near to "thousands upon thousands of angels in joyful assembly." Just as God Himself is not far away, neither are His holy angels. They surround the people of God, watching us with great interest, observing our progress in the Christian faith, standing by to help us when we are in great distress. Sometimes they intervene in subtle ways, sometimes in dramatic, miraculous fashion to deliver God's people.

It is right at this point that angels become so important to us. *We are a dying race living on a dying planet.* All that we see around us will someday vanish without a trace. Despite our best efforts, there is nothing we can do to save ourselves. If we are to be saved, salvation must come from somewhere else.

The angels bring good news of great joy, the best news the world has ever heard.

There are more miracles to come. The fact we do not see them does not mean they are not there. Without the angels of God, we would not survive another day. Thank God for the holy angels who deliver God's people in times of trouble.

My Father, I thank You for the angels,
those unseen messengers from heaven who
encamp around the righteous. Thank You for
protecting me in ways I will never know
until I finally get to heaven. Amen.

1. Name four ways angels protect and help God's people.
2. After reading 2 Kings 6:8–17, what does it suggest about the angelic hosts who surround you today?
3. How is this different than how angels are presented in pop culture?

THE CHANGING SEASONS OF LIFE

The moon marks off the seasons,
and the sun knows when to go down.

PSALM 104:19

Happy are they who find joy in every season of life.

I received a letter from a friend who detailed some of the challenges facing her family right now. The specifics are personal and private, but the trials are real and not likely to go away any time soon. She added this PS to her letter:

> I was listening to Moody radio and Tony Evans' wife was talking about things and situations God allows us to go through. She suggested we just rest in God and let him take us through 'our Season.' This is Fall Season, my favorite time of the year … ironic, with all that I am going through … but I know I'll be fine, because God is taking me through the 'Season' that he has prepared for me. Praise him.

The seasons of the year are first mentioned in Genesis 1:14 as part of the creation week. Psalm 104:19 reminds us the sun and the moon help us mark the passage of time: "The moon marks off the seasons, and the sun knows when to go down." Birds of the air have a God-given ability to change with the times: "Even the stork in the sky knows her appointed seasons, and the dove, the swift and the thrush observe the time of their migration" (Jer. 8:7). Daniel confidently proclaimed that God's sovereignty encompasses time and circumstance when he declared, "Praise be to the name of God for ever and ever; wisdom and power are His. He changes times and seasons; He sets up kings and deposes them" (Dan. 2:20–21). Acts 14:17 reminds us the changing seasons are a gift from above: "He has shown kindness by giving you rain from heaven and crops in their seasons."

Lois Evans was right. Just as there are seasons of the year, there are also God-ordained seasons of life. We know the obvious ones—birth, childhood, youth, young adulthood, the middle years, the later years, and the final years. And there is grade school, high school, college and beyond, singleness, marriage, children, the empty nest, grandchildren, and for some there is singleness a second time. There are jobs and careers, new homes and moves to distant places.

Often there is success, sometimes there is failure. Friendships formed, nurtured, treasured, and sometimes broken, sometimes restored. There are seasons of health and seasons of sickness, seasons of certainty and seasons of doubt. There are happy days and long, lonely nights.

If you live long enough, you will experience most of these and much more. Solomon reminded us of this truth in his famous passage about "a time to be born and a time to die" (Eccles. 3:1–8).

God knows where you are today, and He knows where you will be tomorrow.

Lord Jesus, You have given me much that I do not deserve. I pray for the gift of contentment so I might enjoy this season of my life because it too is a gift from You. Amen.

1. What season of life are you in right now?
2. What lessons do you think the Lord wants to teach you?
3. What does contentment look like in this season of your life?

OUR WORK IS OUR MINISTRY

Then man goes out to his work,
to his labor until evening.
PSALM 104:23

How we work is as crucial as how we pray.

There is no greater testimony than the Christian mechanic at the bench, the Christian teacher in the classroom, the Christian secretary at the desk, the Christian nurse at the hospital, or the Christian accountant keeping the books.

Our problem is that we don't see our daily work as a way to worship God. But it is. What you do on Monday is as sacred as what you do on Sunday. Since most of our lives are spent working to earn our bread, we ought to see our work as an extension of our worship of God. If we cannot be holy at our work, it is useless to attempt to be holy elsewhere. Someone has said, "It is a terrible thing for religious people to have nothing to do but be religious." And again, "Those who get up in the morning with nothing to do but be religious are generally a great nuisance."

The man who gets up in the morning, goes to his job, and works all day in the marketplace, and the woman who cheerfully pursues her daily tasks at home or in the workplace—these are the ones who make an impact for Christ in the world.

The lowliest occupation becomes a powerful sermon

when it is done with dignity, propriety, honesty, diligence, and faithfulness. The common man who does his common job with uncommon grace will never lose his self-respect and will win respect for the church of Jesus Christ.

Martin Luther King, Jr. put this way:

> Whatever your life's work is, do it well. … A man should do his job so well that the living, the dead, and the unborn could do it no better. If it falls your lot to be a street sweeper, sweep streets like Michelangelo painted pictures, like Shakespeare wrote poetry, like Beethoven composed music; sweep streets so well that all the host of Heaven and earth will have to pause and say, "Here lived a great street sweeper, who swept his job well."

Remember, you are the only Bible someone will ever read. You are the only gospel someone will ever hear. You are the only Christian someone will ever meet. What do people read, hear, and see when they look at your life?

Someone has said that, "the only way to show that Christianity is the best of all faiths is to show that it produces the best of all men." When Christians show that our faith makes us better workers, truer friends, better neighbors, kinder men and women, then we are really preaching. Our lives are sermons that daily draw others to Jesus—or push them away from Him.

God of all my days, give me strength
to do the work You have put before me.
When I am tempted to be lazy, remind
me that You are always watching me.
Let my work be my worship today. Amen.

1. Do you agree your work is a major part of your spiritual witness?
2. Have you ever known a Christian who gave a poor testimony because of poor work habits?
3. Take a moment to pray your work will be an effective "sermon" today.

THE CHURCH'S SECRET WEAPON

Glory in his holy name;
let the hearts of those who
seek the Lord *rejoice.*

PSALM 105:3

"Prayer is not everything,
but everything is by prayer." - Ray Ortlund

All Christians would agree with that statement. No matter what our background, we instinctively know prayer is central to the Christian life.

How important is prayer? Let Corrie ten Boom answer that question: "When a Christian shuns fellowship with other Christians, the devil smiles. When he stops reading the Bible, the devil laughs. When he stops praying, the devil shouts for joy."

Acts 1:14 explains why the early church saw explosive growth. The first Christians were "all joined together constantly in prayer." This prayer meeting came after the Ascension and before the descent of the Spirit on the Day of Pentecost. They prayed together for ten days, and it was out of that prayer meeting that unity came.

That, of course, is the point.

It's an odd thing, isn't it? It's hard to pray for people you don't like and don't trust. And it's also hard to pray for people and still not like them. Either you'll stop hating them and start loving them or you'll keep hating and stop praying.

One leads to the other, and praying together for mutual concerns brings a church together like nothing else can. The glue of the church is not its pastor, its program, its buildings, or its doctrine. *United prayer is the glue that makes a church stick together.*

A friend told me he had visited the Brooklyn Tabernacle, a church with a dynamic ministry in a difficult urban setting. Each week the church ministers to thousands of people. It has excellent Bible teaching, great music, warm fellowship. But my friend reported that the Tuesday night prayer meeting draws the largest crowd each week. No wonder the church is growing.

During a visit to a mission station in Belize, God impressed on my heart that if the church I pastor was going to go to the next level, we would only get there through prayer. The Lord clearly said we wouldn't get there by preaching, programs, or publicity. Prayer must be the key.

The Christian church was born in a prayer meeting. Those who study the great spiritual awakenings tell us that without exception, all of them have been preceded by times of united prayer. It's a good sign in any church when believers make prayer a priority.

Let us therefore repeat it once again—prayer is the key. Acts 2:42 tells us the early disciples "devoted themselves to … prayer." Is it any wonder that as a result God gave them unity, miracles, and thousands of people coming to Christ?

All things are possible when a church prays.

Lord Jesus, may my church become a house of prayer—and grant that I might become a praying Christian. Amen.

1. What place does prayer have in your own church?
2. Why is united prayer so important?
3. Name three good things that happen when believers pray together.

KEEP HOPE ALIVE

He remembers his covenant forever, the word he commanded, for a thousand generations, the covenant he made with Abraham.

PSALM 105:8–9

Where is God stretching your faith right now?

An old man and an old woman, childless for decades, are promised by God that someday they would have a baby. Abraham responds with total honesty. He laughs out loud at the Almighty. When Sarah hears the news, she laughs, too. How could such a thing happen? Twenty-five long years pass while they wait for God to keep His promise. Now he is 99 and she is 89. Surely they have hoped in vain. Suddenly, when it seems like all hope is gone, God intervenes with an amazing announcement: By this time next year, you will have a child. Somehow God imparts life to two tired, worn-out bodies, and one year later a son is born. His name is Isaac, which means "laughter."

Abraham was 75 when God made the promise; he was 100 when Isaac was born. When you think about it, there's only one way Abraham could have kept on believing for all those years. He was God-centered, not man-centered. His life had a vertical focus, not a horizontal focus. As long as he looked at his circumstances, he could find a thousand reasons to give up:

"I'm too old."

"She's too old."

"Nothing like this has ever happened before."

"We have tried to have a baby for years and it hasn't worked."

"Our friends think we're nuts."

His only hope was to believe the promise of God. He did … and after 25 years his faith was rewarded. How did he do it? Romans 4:18 says, "Against all hope, Abraham in hope believed." This is always where faith meets the acid test. Are you willing to believe God even when the outward circumstances argue against it? Abraham was. Where would he find any encouragement? From his friends? Forget it. From Sarah? She thought it was a cruel joke. From his father, Terah? He was dead. From his nephew, Lot? Not a chance. So where would he get encouragement? Not from any human being living or dead. Abraham had no one to encourage him. No one except God.

That leads me to ask a simple question. Where is God stretching your faith right now? Where would it be easier for you to doubt God than to believe Him? As you think about those questions, ponder the story of Abraham and Sarah. God put it in the Bible for at least two reasons: So that we will know God always keeps His promises. So that we will never stop believing even though we have to wait a long time for God to answer our prayers.

Keep hope alive. You never know what God will do.

Lord Jesus, teach me to trust You even when my heart is filled with doubt. Amen.

1. Name a few reasons why Abraham and Sarah might have doubted God's promise?
2. How did they keep hope alive?
3. Where is God stretching your faith today?

THE BENEFITS OF PAIN

Then they cried to the LORD in their trouble,
and he saved them from their distress.
PSALM 107:19

God often reveals Himself to us in a crisis situation.

My youngest son and I journeyed back home to surprise my mother on her seventy-fifth birthday. It was the first time my brothers and I had gotten together in seven years. We truly did surprise her, and that was worth the entire trip.

While I was in town, someone I did not know asked to meet with me. I agreed, and I ended up spending about an hour talking with a woman whose marriage was on the verge of total collapse.

The names were new, but the story was old. After twenty years of marriage, her husband was bored and frustrated. So, he moved out to live by himself. She wanted to make the marriage work, but more than that, she wanted to know God better. Could I help her?

She put it this way. "For twenty years my husband has been the center of my life. Now that he's left, I've discovered I can't build my life around him. For the first time, I've learned Jesus Christ must be the center of my life."

I told her two things: "First, I can't guarantee your husband will come back. He might or he might not, and there's nothing you can do to guarantee your marriage will survive.

Second, you're going to be all right as long as you keep seeking the Lord. You've been asking God to show Himself to you in a new way. That's a prayer God will always answer."

God often reveals Himself to us in a crisis situation. Not long after that trip, I spoke with a woman whose godly husband died at a relatively young age, leaving her with several children to raise. Through her tears she spoke of how much she has learned about God in the weeks since her husband's death. She would not ask to have him back in exchange for the things God has taught her about Himself. So it is that we learn more in the shadows than in the sunlight.

None of us would choose to go through a crisis to learn more about God. We rarely have a choice. But we do have a choice about whether we will learn from a crisis and use it as an opportunity to grow closer to God. Hard times come to all of us sooner or later. If our hearts are open, through our tears we can learn more about our heavenly Father than we ever knew before.

Almighty God, help me to respond graciously to the unexpected things that will happen to me today. Amen.

1. How much is knowing God worth to you?
2. Who or what is the center of your life right now?
3. Take a moment to thank God for revealing Himself to you through the hard times of life.

WHERE WISDOM BEGINS

The fear of the Lord *is the beginning of wisdom; all who follow his precepts have good understanding.*

PSALM 111:10

Holy living is motivated by a godly fear.

The "fear of the Lord" is a major biblical theme in both testaments. It is the key to long life, wisdom, prosperity, knowledge, and happiness. It is the most important quality a father can hand down to his children.

Two other Old Testament verses clarify what it is:

(1) *It is an attitude of the heart.* "Oh, that their hearts would be inclined to fear me and keep all my commands always, so that it might go well with them and their children forever!" (Deut. 5:29).

(2) *It is a choice.* "They hated knowledge and did not choose to fear the Lord" (Prov. 1:29).

What is the fear of the Lord? It is the personal choice of respectful love that makes you want to do the things that please Him. It is not cringing fear. That's respect without love. It's also not irreverent flippancy. That can be love without respect.

The fear of the Lord is not the opposite of love. It's what real love is all about. It is the basis of a healthy relationship with God. When I choose to fear the Lord, I choose out of respect and love to do the things that please Him. All that I do in my life comes back to this.

Fearing God means taking Him seriously. That's why the fear of the Lord is where holiness begins. In a world where most people take God lightly, anyone who takes God seriously will stand out as different, separate, distinct. That's what the word *holy* means.

What are the marks of those who take God seriously? They avoid evil, have a tender conscience, are eager to know what pleases God, and guard against temptation.

This answers many questions: What made the saints of old stand strong in the face of persecution, suffering, and torture? They feared God more than they feared man. What makes single mothers keep bringing their children to church week after week? They take God seriously. What makes a businessman refuse a promotion that would take him away from his family and his church? He takes God seriously. What gives teenagers the courage to just say no? They take God seriously.

What makes a woman give up a lucrative career as a surgeon to serve God in Nigeria? She takes God seriously. What makes a young couple decide to become foster parents? They take God seriously. What is it that makes a fellow get up early to read the Bible and pray? Nothing more than this: He takes God seriously.

Why do some Christians keep praying year after year for others to be saved? Because they take God seriously. Why do parents dedicate their children in front of the congregation? Because they take God seriously.

Here is the truth in one sentence: Holy living is motivated by a godly fear that does not take lightly what was purchased at so great a cost.

Holy Father, I pray my life may show
that godly fear and great joy spring from
the same eternal fountain. Amen.

1. Define in practical terms what it means to "fear the Lord."
2. Would a person watching your life conclude that you take God seriously?
3. Why is the fear of the Lord the "beginning" of wisdom?

THE HEALING POWER OF KIND WORDS

Even in darkness light dawns for the upright,
for the gracious and compassionate and righteous man.
PSALM 112:4

When it comes to how we use our words,
there is a better way.

I tell this same story in my book *Finding Wisdom in Proverbs*, and I think it applies here too. One of my seminary professors liked to remind us that "it takes no size to criticize." I often think about that when I am tempted to take cheap shots at other people. The world is filled with critics. Where are the affirmers? On every hand we have self-appointed "truth-tellers" whose calling in life seems to be finding what's wrong with everyone else. If you listen to them long enough they'll soon begin sniping at others.

But there is a better way. I picked up a copy of the Four-Way Test. It consists of four questions to ask yourself when tempted to say something unkind.

1. Is it the truth?
2. Is it fair to all concerned?
3. Will it build goodwill and better friendships?
4. Will it be beneficial to all concerned?

It's pretty simple, isn't it? What a difference it would make if we applied those four questions this week.

Proverbs 18:21 says, "The tongue has the power of life and death." Think about that. Every time you open your mouth either life or death comes out. What has been coming out of your mouth this week? Life or death?

Some people can't keep friends because they speak death into every relationship. They are so critical and petty that they kill every friendship they have. Many marriages die because we kill them with our unkind words. Some families fall apart because the parents kill their children with harsh words. The same can be true where we work. We destroy our team spirit through backbiting, gossip, slander, and lying.

What do these things bring to a relationship?

- Death in our lips
- A corpse in our mouth
- The stench of the grave in our words

But the other side is also true. We may give life by the things we say.

- Positive words
- Hopeful comments
- Life-giving affirmations

Here is the bottom line: When we affirm others, God affirms them through us, and His name is honored. As one writer put it, "God becomes believable as we become lovable." We know this is not a fanciful connection since the last phrase of Psalm 112:4 is applied to God in Psalm 111:4.

As Spurgeon pointed out, when God makes a man upright, He makes him like Himself. As we open our lips to speak words of kindness, the Spirit of Christ goes with our words and uses them to point men and women to God.

May my lips, O Lord, be the very lips of
Jesus—filled with grace and truth. Amen.

1. Are you a critic—or an affirmer?
2. How much "death" has come out of your mouth in the last three days?
3. Pray that God would help you speak life into every situation you encounter today.

HE DOES WHATEVER PLEASES HIM

Our God is in heaven;
he does whatever pleases him.

PSALM 115:3

Life is hard, but God is good.

It was late, and I was working on my sermon in my basement office. I rarely have visitors to my office at home, and no one ever drops by on Saturday night. But on this particular night, I heard a knock at the door. When I opened it, there stood an old friend with tears streaming down his face. As he walked in and sat down, he kept repeating two words: "It's over." I knew what he meant. His marriage was coming to a very sad end. Although both he and his wife were Christians, a series of sinful choices had brought their marriage to a total collapse. That night she told him she was filing for divorce. My friend sat in my office, tears coursing down his cheeks, thoroughly broken as he realized that soon his marriage would be over, and he would be divorced.

He said two things had sustained him in this agonizing personal crisis. The first one was a song on the local Christian station: "Life Is Hard, but God Is Good." He had heard it so many times he knew the words by heart. And he had discovered through his pain that both parts of the title were true. Life *is* hard. No one had to convince him of that. But as he contemplated the wreckage of a marriage he had hoped would last forever, he was discovering that even in his pain, God *is* good.

Then he said he had learned a verse of Scripture that had helped him greatly. It was Psalm 115:3, "Our God is in heaven; He does whatever pleases Him." On the surface, that might seem a strange verse for such a sad moment, yet it had been a lifeline to him. *The truth of God's sovereignty and God's freedom meant that what was happening to him was part of the outworking of God's plan.* Though human sin had caused it, God had allowed it to come, and He did not intervene to stop it. Therefore, God would help him through it, and in the end, he would learn many painful and much-needed lessons.

That happened a number of years ago. *Looking back, my friend would say today he believes that verse even more than he did then.* Nothing happens anywhere in the universe by accident. There is no such thing as luck or fate or chance. God is at work in all things at all times to accomplish His will in the universe. He does whatever pleases Him.

When we submit ourselves to our heavenly Father and finally say, "Lord, You are God and I am not," when we bow before Him, through our tears if necessary, then (and only then) do we discover true freedom. This is what Jesus meant when He said, "You will know the truth, and the truth will set you free" (John 8:32).

Those whom the Son sets free are free indeed.

Almighty God, increase my faith so that I might believe without wavering that You are greater than all my problems. Amen.

1. How do you know that "God is able" to meet your needs?
2. In times of difficulty, why is your starting point all important?
3. Take a moment to thank God for His mighty power.

LET THE NATIONS REJOICE!

Praise the Lord, all you nations;
extol him, all you peoples.

PSALM 117:1

Praise is the universal language of the Christian church.

I have discovered to my delight that God has His people scattered in some very unusual places, and I have learned there are many different ways to worship God in spirit and in truth. I learned to do a little worship dance at the YWAM base in Belize. Along with my friend John Sergey, I observed a Greek Orthodox liturgy in St. Petersburg, Russia. I clapped and cheered with enthusiastic Haitian believers during an evangelistic campaign. I have preached in an evangelical church on the banks of the Volga River and joined in worship with the King of Kings church in Jerusalem.

When we visited Jos, Nigeria, a few years ago, the church we attended took a special offering for the building fund. They called people to come forward by groups and put their offerings in a big metal tub in the front of the church. So, while we all stood and clapped and sang, the different groups came forward singing and dancing, bringing their offerings with them. When the time came for the church leaders to come forward, I went with them, dancing as I went forward with my offering. My dancing wasn't much more than shuffling my feet, and I wasn't very good at that, but I did it, and I enjoyed it. God has continually pulled me out of my comfort zone in the last few years to show me that his family is much bigger than I ever imagined.

I have sung "Just As I Am" with forty-five thousand others at a Billy Graham Crusade in Denver, listened with awe to the magnificent sound of "Holy, Holy, Holy" on a pipe organ, stood around a campfire in Schroon Lake, New York, with three hundred teenagers singing "We Are Climbing Jacob's Ladder," and heard the beautiful chanting of the Catholic monks at the Church of the Holy Sepulcher in Jerusalem. On a trip to Paraguay, my wife and I learned to sing "Hay Vida" in Spanish and one or two songs in the Guarani language.

When we get to heaven, we will all praise the Lamb together—redeemed saints from every nation, tongue, tribe, race, culture, and ethnic group on the face of the earth. Together we will worship Him in unending praise around the throne of God. In that day it won't be one style or language over another. It will simply be heavenly praise to Jesus.

What a wonderful day that will be.

Until then we will worship Him in different ways, but if those ways are acceptable to God, they must be acceptable to us also. In that spirit let us move forward with joy, with enthusiasm, with excitement, not judging each other or putting each other down, but celebrating the fact that we are still one church, one body, one family of God. We're not all alike, but we are one people.

Lord Jesus, hasten the day when all Your children will worship You with one voice around the throne of God. Amen.

1. Make your own list of the different worship experiences you have had.
2. What does that teach you about God's intention for His people?
3. Why do we argue about worship styles?

THE KING IS COMING!

Blessed is he who comes in the name of the L*ORD*.
From the house of the L*ORD we bless you.*

PSALM 118:26

A "Holy Hurrah"

You've heard this verse before. All four gospels quote this verse in connection with Christ's triumphal entry into Jerusalem. The gospel writers make a point to mention what the people shouted.

First, people cried out, "Hosanna! Hosanna! Hosanna!" Then they said, "Blessed is He who comes in the name of the Lord."

"Hosanna!" is a Hebrew word meaning "Save us now." As one writer put it, "Hosanna!" was kind of like a "Holy Hurrah." Every observant Jew immediately recognized the second statement as a quotation from Psalm 118. They all knew it because Psalm 118 was one of the best-known messianic psalms.

By shouting these words, the people were explicitly identifying Jesus as the promised Messiah. No other meaning could reasonably be construed from their exultant shouts. These people believed that at long last the Messiah had come.

They were right.

The Messiah had come—in person, riding on the foal

of a donkey. Sometimes it is overlooked that Jesus gladly accepted the praise of the people on Palm Sunday. What a change this was. For most of His public ministry, whenever He worked a miracle, He told people not to spread the word. Perhaps it was because He wanted people to see Him as more than a miracle worker. But not that day. The time for silence was long past. If He once discouraged publicity, He now counted silence inconceivable.

The time for truth had come. When the Pharisees heard the crowds praising Him, they urged Him to rebuke His disciples. Jesus refused, saying, "If I tell them to be quiet, the rocks themselves will break forth in praise to Me."

Later that week, as His crucifixion drew near, Jesus confronted the Pharisees about their utter hypocrisy. After pronouncing seven "woes" upon them, He declared that Jerusalem would not see Him again until the people said, "Blessed is He who comes in the name of the Lord" (Matt. 23:39).

Here is a solemn reminder of history's greatest mistake. The King had come to His people, and His people had put Him to death. But there is also in these words an implicit promise—"you will see Me again."

He came once as the Lamb of God. He will return as the Lion of the tribe of Judah. And in that day, the nation of Israel will see Him as He is, and "all Israel will be saved" (Rom. 11:26). That day is yet future to us, and no one can say when it will come. May it be soon.

Even so, come Lord Jesus.

Lord Jesus, You promised to return.
Today wouldn't be too soon. If not today,
then tomorrow. Help me to live so that
I won't be surprised or ashamed when
that glad day finally arrives. Amen.

1. Do you expect Jesus to return in your lifetime?
2. In what ways is the Second Coming the "blessed hope" of the believer?
3. Are you ready for His return?

HOW TO STAY CLEAN IN A DIRTY WORLD

How can a young man keep his way pure?
By living according to your word.

PSALM 119:9

Tattoo God's Word on your heart.

Let me tell you a story about how this verse works. A young man came to see me because he struggled to keep his thought life pure. Though he was bold about his faith on the job, he felt utterly defeated because of his ongoing struggles to achieve moral purity. "I want to be married someday, but how can I be a Christian husband when I'm not the man I want to be right now?" As I talked to him, I sensed two things that gave me hope—his utter honesty and a deep-seated desire to do whatever it took to put his life on a new course. I challenged him to begin memorizing Scripture. He seemed skeptical that it would make any difference, and I told him that his life would not change overnight.

Where should he begin? I suggested that he start with Psalm 119. For those who don't know, that's the longest chapter in the Bible—176 verses—and it's all about the power of God's Word.

Few people would have the courage to tackle such a

huge project, and fewer still would finish. Almost everyone would burn out after ten or twenty or thirty verses. But I suspected that this young man was different.

He left my office with a promise that he would start and that he would check in with me from time to time. Over the next few weeks, when I saw him in church, I would ask him how he was doing.

It took him ten full months to memorize all of Psalm 119. Finally, the day came when he sat in my office and said, "Check me out." I sat and followed along in my Bible as he recited all 176 verses. It was an amazing experience for me to hear this young man recite God's Word with so much confidence and so much joy. Something had clearly happened inside his heart as the Word had taken root. From time to time, he would stop and comment on how powerful this verse was or how much that verse meant to me or what amazing truth this verse contained.

Clearly, he had memorized more than words on paper. The life-giving Word of God had entered his soul. And all that Psalm 119 promises had come true in his life. He quite simply was not the defeated man who walked into my office ten months earlier. The Word had done its work. That was many years ago. He continued to memorize Scripture.

Today, he is married to a wonderful Christian woman, and together, they are raising their family for the Lord. He would say that memorizing Scripture changed his life.

Why should this surprise us? Psalm 119:130 says, "The unfolding of your words gives light."

Try it and see for yourself. Tattoo God's Word on your heart, and you'll be amazed at how it changes your life.

Spirit of the Living God, cleanse me from the inside out so that my passion becomes a pure stream, not a polluted river. Amen.

1. Make a list of the people who are depending on you to make wise choices.
2. What is the best argument you know for staying morally pure?
3. What Bible verse has God pressed on your heart to memorize?

A QUIET TIME AT THE RIGHT TIME

Open my eyes that I may see
wonderful things in your law.
PSALM 119:18

The Word is energized within us as we believe it.

I first learned this verse more than half a century ago when a Christian college professor used it as his theme verse for our course in Old Testament Survey. Dr. Wymal Porter encouraged us to make this verse our prayer as we studied the fascinating history of God's dealings with Israel. Ever since then it has reminded me that I must pray for God's illumination, for without it I am just reading words on paper.

This verse also reminds us that the Word of God has power when its divine authority is accepted in a believing heart. It is like farmland that bears a rich harvest, like a gold mine that delivers great riches, or like an investment that pays a huge dividend. When our eyes are opened to see the "wonderful things" in God's Word, it comes alive within us and produces a bountiful harvest.

The summer after learning this verse, I served as a counselor at Word of Life Island in Schroon Lake, New York, where I was exposed for the first time to a concept called "the quiet time." A quiet time means setting aside a few minutes each day to read the Bible and pray. The people at Word of Life were so committed to it that they set aside thirty minutes every day when the whole camp stopped, and we all went off and had a quiet time. We even had a little diary that we filled in with our thoughts and prayers.

Some people would call it devotions, others the morning watch. It makes no difference what title you use. Since then, I have read hundreds of books on the spiritual life. When all is said and done, I know nothing more important for maintaining a warm relationship with Jesus Christ than a consistent, regular, quality quiet time.

It has not gotten easier over the years. In many ways, it has gotten harder. It almost always does because we tend to substitute our knowledge and Christian activity for this simple discipline of spending time daily with God and His Word.

I commend to you the practice of a daily quiet time. How can we say we believe the Bible and accept its authority if we do not daily spend time in the Word? If you are an elder or a deacon or a deaconess, if you attend a Christian college or if you work for a Christian organization, if you have been a Christian for many years, if you teach Sunday school or serve the Lord in some way, don't say your knowledge makes a quiet time unnecessary.

New Christians rarely have to be convinced about this. Experienced Christians often forget this truth and suffer spiritually as a result.

Eternal Father, let Your Word be planted deep in my heart today that it may bring forth a harvest of righteousness in my life. Amen.

1. Do you agree that a daily time with the Lord is important for your spiritual growth?
2. How consistent are you in this area?
3. Memorize Psalm 119:18 and then share it with a friend.

THE FRATERNAL ORDER OF CHRISTIAN STRANGERS

I am a stranger on earth; do not hide your commands from me.

PSALM 119:19

Salvation has made you a stranger in the world.

I am writing these words in Miango, Nigeria, on the final night of a thirteen-day visit with some missionary friends. It doesn't take long to understand what it means to be a stranger in a strange land. You will never know what it's like until you visit a foreign country and there see people who don't look like you, talk like you, think like you, or live like you.

They have a set of values you don't understand, a language you can't speak, and food you can't eat. You pick up the newspaper, and you can't read it. You turn on the radio, and it doesn't make sense. You're standing on a sidewalk, and you can't communicate with the people who pass by. And no matter how friendly the people are, you never forget, not even for one second, that you are an outsider.

If you follow Jesus, you have become a stranger—not in some other country but in your own hometown. It's like going back to the place where you grew up only to find out that everything has changed, and nothing looks the same.

You didn't move physically, but you did move spiritually.

If you are a businessman and have decided as a Christian not to cheat, lie, or double-cross, if you've decided to deliver what you promise, you are a stranger in the world.

If you are a husband and you have decided to be faithful to your wife because you are a Christian, you are a stranger in the world.

If you are a Christian teenager, and you have decided to live for Jesus in the halls of your high school, you are a resident alien.

If you have decided to do your work as unto the Lord, not as pleasing men but to please God, if you have decided that money will not be the determining factor in your life, then you are a stranger in the world.

If you work in an office where coarse language, profanity, and loose talk are the accepted norm and you have decided not to join in, you are a stranger in the world.

If any of those things are true, then welcome to the fraternal order of Christian strangers. You are an alien in this world because you are a citizen of heaven. Don't be discouraged if you sometimes feel out of place. You're not home yet.

Lord of the cloud and fire, I am a pilgrim marching through the wilderness on my way to the Promised Land. When I am discouraged and want to go back to Egypt, keep my feet marching toward Canaan. Amen.

1. In what sense are Christians "strangers in a strange land"?
2. According to Philippians 3:20–21, where is your true citizenship?
3. What makes you feel like a stranger in the world?

COMPANIONS ON THE ROAD TO HEAVEN

I am a friend to all who fear you,
to all who follow your precepts.
PSALM 119:63

Are you familiar with the term *cocooning*?

Experts use the word *cocooning* to describe contemporary American life. It refers to the fact that Americans are using their homes as a way to escape contact with the world. Cocooning is what happens when you use your home like a medieval castle. You let down the drawbridge, go to work, come home, cross the drawbridge, raise it, and fill the moat with water. You sit down, turn on the TV, read the paper, and then go to bed. The next day you do it all over again.

One result of cocooning is that people don't get to know others. They never let anyone get close enough. Only the special few get invited across the drawbridge. Everyone else is, "Hi, how are you? It's good to see you. Sorry I don't have time to talk. I have to run. Bye-bye."

God never intended that His children live in cocoons. He designed Christian life not to be a solo, but a duet, a trio, a quartet, a quintet, a choir, and a mighty symphony. He intended that as you join your life with other people, they would help you and you would help them. It's not easy to live this way, because it runs against the grain of contemporary culture.

Although we hunger for close relationships, we live in a way that makes it easier to keep things superficial. We move too much, don't know how to talk to each other, are too busy, and are unwilling to commit ourselves to long-term relationships.

You may be struggling right now because you don't have a group, are not close to anyone, and are not accountable to anybody. God didn't create a race of hermits.

He intended that His children would live together, and that in living together, they would help each other along the way. It is God's will that we live together as brothers and sisters in a family relationship so that we can love each other, encourage each other, admonish each other, hug each other, pick each other up when we fall down, rejoice together, weep together, and correct each other when we make mistakes.

How is it with you? Do you have a few people in your life who really know you? Or do you always wear the mask, wear the costume, play the game, because the show must go on? Are you accountable to anybody for the way you live? Or are you doing it all by yourself?

Lord God, thank You for the gift of Christian friends. Help me to be a friend to my friends today. Amen.

1. How many truly close friends do you have?
2. Which relationships need your attention?
3. What can you do about them this week?

FOREVER SETTLED IN HEAVEN

Your word, O Lord, is eternal;
it stands firm in the heavens.
PSALM 119:89

God never asks us to correct His Word.

This verse demonstrates why the battle over the nature of the Bible is so crucial. If it is only the word of man, then it is changeable, fickle, and unreliable. But if the Bible is the Word of God, then it is utterly and completely authoritative. If God has spoken in the Bible, then what He says has final claim on my life.

Let me summarize this point with two simple statements:

1. If the Bible comes from man, we are entitled to sit in judgment on it.
2. If the Bible comes from God, we must bow in submission to it.

This is a crucial question: What do you believe about the Bible? Does it come from man or from God? Is it on the level with the daily newspaper, or does it speak with divine authority?

If you say it is the Word of God, then you must also say

that it is not simply one message among many. It is not like the Republican or the Democratic platform that come about through debate and consensus. If the Bible is the Word of God, it is utterly exclusive in its claims. It does not beg for our approval. The Word of God is not like the first draft of a thesis that the writer submits and asks, "What do you think?"

A friend in Texas sent me an e-mail saying that he had just received the first two chapters of his dissertation back from the seminary library. They covered his pages with red marks. Change this, delete that, follow a different form in your footnotes, use this kind of paper, indent this many spaces, and so on. He has to do what they say if he wants to get his degree.

Not so with the Bible. God never asks us to correct His Word. He never asks us to review Isaiah and make a few changes. And He won't abide by those who add to or take away from the book of Revelation (22:18–19).

It reminds me of the story of a church that was going through a difficult controversy. No one could agree on anything. At a business meeting one night, the various factions were arguing about the minutes of the previous meeting. When the pastor read a passage of Scripture, an old man stood to his feet and said, "Mr. Chairman, I move that the Bible stand approved as read."

So it must be for you and me. The Bible is approved as read, without correction, change, deletion, or addition.

O Lord, may I never doubt Your Word, but simply believe it, obey it, and build my life upon it. Amen.

1. How do you know the Bible is the Word of God?
2. Why is the doctrine of inerrancy (that the Bible is without error in all its details) so crucial for our faith?
3. Spend some time thanking God for giving us the Bible.

DO YOU LOVE GOD'S WORD?

Oh, how I love your law!
I meditate on it all day long.

PSALM 119:97

How do you love a book of laws?

The very idea of loving the law seems to be an oxymoron—two words that don't normally go together. For instance, suppose I go to a Driver's License Bureau and pick up the "Rules of the Road."

It's basically a set of laws governing how we should drive. So, as I read it, I begin to say to myself, "I love this book. I love the rules about no passing on a hill. I love the law that covers parallel parking. And I really love the regulations for getting your license renewed."

Most people would think that a little strange. And they would be right. So, let's try that illustration another way. Suppose you buy a Betty Crocker cookbook. When I ask you how you like it, you tell me, "I love this cookbook. I love everything about it. I love the way it looks and feels. But I really love the recipe for Veal Parmesan. I read it six or seven times a day and when I do, it's hard to keep from crying."

That's also strange.

Now let's make one small change in that illustration. Let's suppose that the recipe book is from your grandmother. Each recipe was written in her own hand and each page is worn and stained from the cooking she did many years ago. As you turn each page and read each recipe, you remember your grandmother and how much she meant to you. You love that recipe book because you loved the person who wrote it. It's more than words on a piece of paper, it's a reminder of a family relationship, a precious symbol of love that spans the generations.

When I think of the Bible that way, the concept of loving God's law takes on new meaning. We love this book because we love the One who wrote this book.

To love God's law means to embrace it wholeheartedly as the rule of your life. Because we love God, we love His Word, and we make it the foundation and the center of all that we do.

As you think about this verse and contemplate what it promises and what it requires, ask God to give you a true and deep and lasting love for His Word. Ask for it. Seek it. Tell the Lord that you want to be more than a reader of the Word and more than a student of the Word. Tell Him you want to love His Word. Ask Him for that love. Pray that it might be implanted in your heart. If we ask in sincerity, that's a prayer God will be pleased to answer.

Lord of all, give me a sincere love for Your Word because it is Your love letter to me. May I love it, believe it, and make it the foundation of my life. Amen.

1. Name someone you know who loves God's Word.
2. What makes them different?
3. What's the difference between reading God's Word and loving it?

MRS. SANDBERG'S ADVICE

Great peace have they who love your law,
and nothing can make them stumble.

PSALM 119:165

Reading God's Word is the pathway to lasting peace.

I learned this verse 50 years ago. It happened in my British Lit. class in college. As Mrs. Sandberg began class one day, she read a verse of Scripture that had been particularly meaningful to her. Then she quoted Psalm 119:165 from the King James Version, "Great peace have they which love Thy law: and nothing shall offend them." I am sure I had never heard that verse before.

Mrs. Sandberg asked us if any of us were having a bad day.

We all have days when things just don't seem to go right, when even nice people get on our nerves, and when we find ourselves easily irritated by things that would normally not bother us. She suggested that when we have a day like that, it might be because we haven't spent time in the Word of God. If we find ourselves easily offended by other people, then we ought to take Psalm 119:165 to heart.

It promises personal security in a topsy-turvy, dangerous, uncertain, and sometimes very hostile world. Nothing we do can change the character of the world. It is what it is. But there is something we can do to keep the world from permanently changing us. God's Word gives us great peace and keeps us upright when everything else turns upside down.

Peace is a wonderful concept, and "great peace" is even better. Peace is man's highest hope and his fondest dream. And most days it seems so hard to achieve. When Christ was born, the angel proclaimed, "Peace on earth, goodwill to men," but after 2,000 years it still seems in short supply.

The Hebrew word for peace is *shalom*. If you visit Israel, people on the street will greet you with "Shalom!" "Peace to you, my friend." It is a mistake to think of *shalom* as simply being the absence of conflict. It is a much richer idea than that. Biblical *shalom* involves things like prosperity, happiness, contentment, and most of all, blessing from the Lord. It is a very rich concept. As J. Oswald Sanders said, "Peace is not the absence of trouble, but the presence of God."

It occurs to me that the only truly happy people I have ever known are those who have prayed, "Thy will be done." They have the "great peace" of Psalm 119:165. They have discovered the way to peace is to yield everything to the Lord. Until you do that, there will be continual inner unrest.

Mrs. Sandberg was right. The only way to have lasting peace is to love God's Word.

Lord, we long for peace but cannot
find it on this sin-cursed planet.
Teach us to love Your Word so
that we might know the great
peace You promise. Amen.

1. Do you have the "great peace" this verse promises?
2. Do you love God's Word?
3. Take a moment and ask God to make this verse come true in your life.

GOD'S LAW OF THE HARVEST

Those who sow in tears will reap with songs of joy. He who goes out weeping, carrying seed to sow, will return with songs of joy, carrying sheaves with him.

PSALM 126:5–6

Farmers understand sowing and faith.

Sowing is always an act of faith. You take your seed, put it in the ground, and cover it with soil. You can't see a thing. One day passes—nothing. Two days pass—nothing. Three days pass—nothing. A week, two weeks—nothing. To the untrained eye, it seems all your planting was for naught.

The farmer may be tempted to think, *I wasted my time. Maybe I shouldn't have planned as much as I did.* It's always that way when you sow. You plant the seed, and then you wait. Once the seed is in the ground, it's too late to change your mind. But if you wait long enough, the harvest comes. Then you are glad you planted as much as you did.

So it is with everything we do for the Lord. Evangelism is like sowing seeds. Not many people come to Christ the first time they hear the message. Like most of us, most people need to think about it, ponder it, ask a few questions, and only later trust Christ. Psalm 126:5–6 encourages us to believe that as we tell others about Christ in the power of the Holy Spirit, God will give the harvest of new believers in His own time and in His own way.

The same principle holds true for our giving, which often seems financially impossible. You've got bills to pay, a heavy mortgage, car payments, dental bills, school bills, maternity clothes to buy, child support payments you have to make. The pantry is almost bare, your youngest daughter needs a new dress, and the poodle needs a pedicure. It looks impossible. You want to give to the Lord, but it seems like throwing seed on the ground. Maybe you should go back. Maybe you should wait. Maybe you can give when you get another raise or when your spouse takes a second job.

But then comes the harvest. It's wonderful to live on a farm during harvest time. All the work of the year begins to pay off. Back from the field comes the truck loaded with corn or wheat or cotton or hay. You don't regret sowing all that seed at harvest time.

That is the great principle: What you give, you end up receiving. This applies in every area of the spiritual life. The generous man receives blessings from God all out of proportion to His own giving. God will be no man's debtor. Those who sow in tears will reap with songs of joy.

Lord of the harvest, grant me the faith to sow in tears, knowing that I shall reap a joyful harvest from Your hand in due time. Amen.

1. Explain the Law of the Harvest.
2. How does it apply to prayer?
3. How does it apply to other areas of the Christian life, such as evangelism, missions, or Bible study?

CHILDREN: A HANDFUL AND A QUIVERFUL

Blessed is the man whose quiver is full of [sons].
They will not be put to shame when they
contend with their enemies in the gate.
PSALM 127:5

How full is your quiver?

This verse seems to teach that large families are a special sign of God's blessing. How full is "full"? The Bible doesn't say, but in every place where it speaks to the subject, children are a sign of God's favor. Not all Bible families were large, of course, but many were.

The city gate was where men of power and influence conducted their business. It was also where wise men ruled and made judgments. Men would meet their adversaries "in the gate." Thus, a father with many sons had many defenders when he was falsely accused.

They could stand and testify to his good name. Note that nothing is said about money or power or position. God's blessing is not seen in worldly wealth or the accumulation of "things" but in a happy family that rallies to the call whenever trouble comes.

It is a striking contrast from a workaholic husband who stays on the road seven days a week and is absent in spirit even when he is home. What shall it profit a man if he gains the whole world and yet loses his own family?

I know many men who spend sixty to seventy hours per week on the job, then in a quiet moment they confide they wish they could spend more time at home. Years later they realize they had all the time they needed, but they used it for other things. Oh, to be wise enough to learn this while there is still time to make a difference.

Derek Kidner makes a valuable point when he reminds us that raising children can be tiresome and difficult. "It is not," he says, "untypical of God's gifts that first they are liabilities ... before they become obvious assets." Children are both a burden and a blessing.

Kidner says, the greater their promise, the more challenging will be the task of raising God's children. Our children will likely be a handful before they become a quiverful.

We can partner with the Lord Jesus Christ in building our homes. When we do, our families will be blessed, our children will prosper, our marriages will flourish, and Jesus Christ will be praised.

We must proclaim the high value of the family, of monogamous marriage, of abstinence before marriage and a happy life together after marriage. We must teach our children that true love waits, that marriage is desirable, that motherhood is a noble calling, and that being a godly father is more important than being an executive VP. We must recapture the truth that our children are worth all the love, all the effort and all the investment of our time and resources.

When we are done with our work on earth, we may look back with joy and say, "God blessed us with a happy Christian family."

There is no greater reward, no better testimony, no higher goal for Christian parents than a family that loves the Lord and each other. If we can say that when the day is done, we may leave this world singing, knowing that we prevailed in the one area of life that matters the most.

O Lord, save me from working so long and
so hard on my career that I lose my family.
I want to work with You in building
a happy Christian home. Amen.

1. Do you agree children are a blessing from the Lord?
2. Why are God's gifts often a liability before they become a blessing?
3. If you have children, take a moment to pray for each one right now.

THE GOD WHO FORGIVES

If you, O Lord, kept a record
of sins, O Lord, who could stand?
But with you there is forgiveness.
PSALM 130:3–4

Can we really be forgiven,
or is forgiveness just a distant dream?

If the Vegas bookies laid odds on our forgiveness, what would the odds be—50,000 to 1, or 100,000 to 1, or maybe even 1,000,000 to 1? Look in the mirror and consider your own soul. If you do, the outlook will not be hopeful. One British writer put it this way: "There is no man who, if all his secret thoughts were made known, would not deserve hanging a dozen times a day."

Sin is real, which means you can't get away with breaking the rules forever. But when you are ready to come clean, the Lord is right there waiting for you. It's never easy to confess your sins, but listen to the invitation God makes in Isaiah 55:7: "Let the wicked forsake his way and the evil man his thoughts. Let him turn to the Lord, and He will have mercy on him, and to our God, for He will freely pardon."

Maybe you don't like the word *wicked* or the word *unrighteous*. Maybe that sounds harsh to you. But that's God's description of the whole human race. That's what we are apart from God's grace. Don't get hung up on the negative words and miss the invitation. Turn to the Lord, and you will find mercy and pardon. The Bible uses many images to describe how God deals with our sins:

- God removes our sins as far as the east is from the west (Ps. 103:12).
- God puts our sins behind His back (Isa. 38:17).
- God blots out our sins like a thick cloud (Isa. 44:22).
- God forgets our sins and remembers them no more (Jer. 31:34).
- God buries our sins in the depths of the sea (Mic. 7:19).

When God forgives our sins, He chooses to forget them forever. Our sins are removed, buried, and blotted out. They can never condemn us again. But how could God forgive us? Why doesn't He look at or remember our sins?

A long time ago, God fixed His gaze on the cross of His Son, the Lord Jesus Christ, who bore our sins. When we are honest enough to admit we are wicked and evil, a stream of mercy flows out from the cross of Christ, and our sins are covered by His blood. We discover in one shining moment that with God there is forgiveness.

If you admit you are a sinner, you can be forgiven. That's the promise God made when He sent His Son to save us from our sins.

Lord Jesus, may the grace that forgave my sins fill my heart so that I may be quick to forgive others when they sin against me. Amen.

1. Why do we need forgiveness?
2. How can we know our sins are forgiven?
3. How many of our sins are forgiven the moment we trust Christ?

HOW GOD WEANS US FROM THE WORLD

But I have stilled and quieted my soul;
like a weaned child with its mother,
like a weaned child is my soul within me.
PSALM 131:2

Only a mother can fully understand this picture.

A child is born, and for a long time, he looks to his mother's breast as the source of his nourishment. Breakfast, lunch, and supper all come from the same place. When he is hungry, he cries, and Mom knows exactly what to do. Her milk satisfies him, and back to sleep he goes.

But the day comes when he has to learn to be satisfied with a bottle.

That's not a happy day. He cries, big tears roll down his face, and his arms reach out, but his mother doesn't give in. He fights, he pouts, he screams, all to no avail. What has happened to Mom? She who used to be his friend has now become his enemy. If Mom has a heart at all, she cries too, because from now on things will be different. She will feed him, but never again in the same way.

Here is the truth: Unless a mother weans her child, he will never grow up. He'll be a baby all the days of his life. Though it may seem hard, and though the child misunderstands, if a mother truly loves her child, she will not stop until the job is fully done. When the job is finally done, the child no longer begs for that which he once found indispensable. Once he could not live without his mother's milk; now he no longer needs it.

At the end of a bloody battle during the Civil War, someone found the following prayer folded in the pocket of dead Confederate soldier:

> I asked God for strength, that I might achieve;
> I was made weak, that I might learn humbly to obey.
> I asked for health, that I might do greater things;
> I was given infirmity, then I might do better things.
> I asked for riches, that I might be happy;
> I was given poverty, that I might be wise.
> I asked for power, that I might have the praise of men;
> I was given weakness, that I might feel the need of God.
> I asked for all things, that I might enjoy life;
> I was given life, that I might enjoy all things.
> I got nothing I asked for, but everything I had hoped for.
> Almost despite myself, my unspoken prayers were
> answered.
> I am, among men, most richly blessed.

David would agree with those sentiments. It is a great advance in spiritual understanding to be able to say, "I got nothing I asked for, but everything I had hoped for."

We ought to be the most thankful people on the face of the earth. May our days be marked with humility, simplicity, and integrity. Let us be thankful not only for the things we have but also for the things we no longer have to have. That, too, is a gift from God.

Lord of my life, wean me from the world
that I might draw my nourishment
from You alone. Amen.

1. Are you a contented person?
2. Is there anything else you need right now to make you truly happy?
3. How has God weaned you from things you once thought you couldn't live without?

WHY WE'RE NOT AFRAID TO DIE

Give thanks to the Lord, *for he is good.*
His love endures forever.

PSALM 136:1

We die, but God's love endures forever.

The call came at 7:30 on Friday morning. A dear friend had died. The end came swiftly. He labored in breathing for about an hour. Then he took two or three breaths, and he was gone. He always said he would fight to the end but that he wouldn't drag it out. It happened just as he predicted. I got to the house about 8:20 to spend time with his wife. There was sorrow but also peace and a sense of relief. She told me that some friends had come by to talk with her husband the night before. The conversation focused on the topic of heaven. They talked about how wonderful heaven is and how good it is to know you are going there. They didn't know my friend would be there in just a few hours.

Jesus told us all about heaven when He said, "In my Father's house are many rooms; if it were not so, I would have told you. I am going there to prepare a place for you. And if I go and prepare a place for you, I will come back and take you to be with me that you also may be where I am" (John 14:2–3).

Do you know the most crucial phrase in that passage? "If it were not so, I would have told you." Our Lord would not lie about a thing like that. He always tells the truth. And when we stand by the grave of a fellow believer, we have to know the truth: Is death the end, or is there something else? "If it were not so, I would have told you."

Each verse of Psalm 136 includes the answering chorus: "His love endures forever." The phrase contains six Hebrew syllables—meant to be chanted out loud—that remind us by their repetition that all things show us God's love at work on behalf of His children.

The word for *love* refers to the loyal love of a covenant relationship, such as the loyalty of a husband to his wife, a father to his children, or a soldier to his country. God's love is eternal because His covenant is eternal. *He cannot not love His people.*

But the thought is more than God's love alone. The Hebrew word emphasizes the fact that God's love endures. It outlasts all the problems of life. It goes beyond the troubles we all face every day. It endures when our life comes to an end. We live and die, but God's love endures forever.

What gives us the confidence to face death with our heads held high? How can we cross the Jordan to reach the other side? We can because "His love endures forever." That's our hope.

We die, but His love endures forever.

We fail, but His love endures forever.

We stumble and fall, but His love endures forever.

We know it because God has said it, Jesus has promised it, and "His love endures forever."

Eternal Lord, thank You for love
that will not let me go. Amen.

1. If you died today, are you sure you would go to heaven?
2. Do you think a person can ever be certain of such a thing?
3. If you answer yes to the first two questions, what is the basis for your answer?

THE UNSTOPPABLE GOD

The Lord *will fulfill his purpose for me;*
your love, O Lord*, endures forever—do not*
abandon the works of your hands.

PSALM 138:8

Your love endures forever.

This little phrase ensures that what God starts, He finishes. It is often said that those who are saved are saved forever. How do we know this is true? We know it because God is faithful to keep His promises.

Our entire hope—both in this life and in the life to come—rests on God's faithfulness. His faithfulness bears the entire weight of our puny efforts. We are saved because of God—and not because of anything we do. He provides the grace that saves us, and He also gives us the faith to believe (Eph. 2:8). He even gives us the Holy Spirit, who gives us the power to obey God.

"The Lord will fulfill His purpose for me." What is "His purpose" for His children? That He would take us where He finds us—as sinners—and that, justifying us even while we are still sinful (see Rom. 5:8), He would set about the lifelong project of conforming us to the image of Jesus Christ (Rom. 8:29).

All of us are works in progress. We're not finished, not glorified, not perfected, not completed. We're all "under construction." Construction is long, loud, noisy, and very messy. That's why most of us can hear hammering and sawing on the inside. God never stops His work because so much work needs to be done. If you concentrate on your weakness, you will lose your confidence. If you concentrate on God's faithfulness, you will grow in confidence.

What makes us think God will finish the job? In my mind's eye, I picture God as a sculptor working with a rough piece of marble. He's working on a big chunk named "Ray Pritchard." It's a hard job because the chunk is badly marred, misshapen, discolored, and cracked in odd places. It's about the worst piece of marble a sculptor could ever find. But God is undeterred, and He works patiently at His job, chipping away the bad parts, chiseling an image into the hard stone, stopping occasionally to polish here and there. One day He finally finishes one section of the statue. The next morning when He returns to the studio that section is messed up. "I thought I finished that yesterday," He says. "Who has been messing with my statue?"

It turns out that I'm the culprit. I'm my own worst enemy. What I thought would improve things has only messed them up.

But God is faithful. He patiently picks up His chisel and goes back to work. He won't quit halfway through a project. What God starts, He finishes. You can take that to the bank.

Heavenly Father, grant me the gift of patience while I wait for You to finish Your work in me. Amen.

1. In what sense are you your own worst enemy?
2. Name several parts of your life where you have seen real spiritual progress in the last several years.
3. Ask God to keep molding you into the image of Jesus Christ.

HERE, THERE, AND EVERYWHERE

Where can I go from your Spirit?
Where can I flee from your presence?

PSALM 139:7

God is present everywhere at all times.

Let's talk about *omnipresence*. That's a big word that means God is present everywhere at all times. This truth has several important implications.

First, He is always present, whether we believe it or not. In the early days of space travel, one of the Russian cosmonauts returned from orbiting the earth to announce that he had looked out his space capsule and had not seen God anywhere. Dr. W. A. Criswell of the First Baptist Church of Dallas replied, "Let him take off his space suit for just one second, and he'll see God quick enough."

Second, He is present even in the worst moments of life. God's omnipresence means that He is there in the midst of suffering, pain, sickness, sorrow, anger, grief, bitterness, divorce, betrayal, murder, rape, sexual abuse, cancer, AIDS, abortion, warfare, famine, earthquakes, fires, floods, every natural disaster, accidents, personal loss, and at the moment of death.

Third, we cannot run from God. When Jacob awoke

from his dream, he exclaimed, "Surely the Lord is in this place, and I was not aware of it" (Gen. 28:16). How typical of us. We think the Lord has forgotten us, but we are the ones who have forgotten Him.

Where is God when we need Him? He's where He's always been, but we didn't know it. You can run away from God to the other side of the earth, and when you get off the plane, He will meet you at baggage claim.

Not everyone meets God in a church service. You are more likely to meet God on the bed of affliction, or when you lose your job, or when your children are sick, or when your friends betray you, or when your marriage collapses. You are more likely to meet Him after the accident than during the coffee hour on Sunday morning.

Often, we don't pay attention to the Lord until tragedy strikes. Then we look up to heaven and say, "Surely the Lord is in this place, and I was not aware of it."

Fourth, we may rely fully on Him no matter how desperate our situation may be. Recently I spoke with two elderly Christian women. One had just been diagnosed with cancer. When I talked with her, she said, "Pastor, don't worry about me. The Lord has been so good to me." She's eighty years old. Later I spoke with a woman who is ninety, very weak and frail and eager to go to heaven. Her voice quivered, but her faith was strong. "I'm just trusting in the Lord," she told me. These dear saints have learned through a lifetime of walking with God that He will never leave them, for He is always present with His people.

Father, thank You for being there whenever we need You even when we don't sense Your presence. Amen.

1. What encouragement do you take from God's promise that "I will never leave you?"
2. How does this truth apply to your prayer life?
3. Is God present even when we don't "feel" Him present with us?

ASKING HARD QUESTIONS

If only you would slay the wicked, O God!
Away from me, you bloodthirsty men!

PSALM 139:19

Love must have limits.

It's easy to skip a verse like this. Perhaps it seems too negative for our taste. After speaking so beautifully about God's presence everywhere (vv. 7–12) and of His creative care of the unborn child (vv. 13–16), and after praising the vastness of God's thoughts (vv. 17–18), why would the psalmist, apparently without warning, shift gears into an attack on His enemies (vv. 19–22)?

Loving the Lord of necessity means hating those who hate the Lord. (Verse 21 says this explicitly.) These are strong words, but entirely true. Not every unbeliever "hates" the Lord, but some do, and their malice must not be underestimated or overlooked.

As a practical way of applying this truth, here are some questions we ought to ask ourselves:

1. Do I really believe the gospel of Jesus Christ?
2. In what areas of my life am I guilty of supporting that which I know is wrong?
3. Have I been silent about evil when I should have been outspoken for the truth?

4. Have I been slowly lowering my standards of right and wrong to maintain friendships or to gain some personal advantage?
5. Have I been dabbling in falsehood when I need to speak up for the truth?
6. Is there a relationship in my life that needs to be broken because it is dragging me down spiritually?
7. If my friends at church could see me during the week, would they be embarrassed by the things I do and say? Would Jesus be embarrassed?

Not easy questions, but ones we need to ask.

Love must have limits. We must love people, but we must not thereby tolerate false doctrine or condone moral evil. To use a familiar phrase, we must love the sinner while hating the sin. Sometimes we may appear to love the sinner too much, and sometimes we may appear to hate the sin too much. Both will be necessary if we are to stand for Christ and win the lost in this evil day.

Perhaps in our tolerance, we have become indifferent to truth. When it comes to eternal issues, there is no room for neutrality. Not every issue is an eternal issue. We can have our own opinions in politics, sports, entertainment, and the latest news of the day. But some things are not up for grabs in the spiritual realm.

Set limits. Ask hard questions. Love God. Hate His enemies. Pray for them—and for yourself that you will maintain a proper attitude.

O Lord, I pray for spiritual balance that I might love the sinner while rejecting the sin that sends sinners to hell. Help me to hope for the best while hating that which destroys the soul. Amen.

1. How would you answer the seven questions in this entry?
2. In practical terms, how can we "love the sinner and hate the sin" at the same time?
3. Name several spiritual truths that are not "up for grabs."

THE FAITH OF A CHILD

Let the morning bring me word of your unfailing love, for I have put my trust in you. Show me the way I should go, for to you I lift up my soul.

PSALM 143:8

Only God could have done it.

A few years ago, a young woman volunteered to serve as a missionary in Africa. Her young nieces had a hard time understanding why their aunt Rachel would be going so far away. While Rachel was in candidate school in California, Beth (who was only four years old) was talking things over with Rachel's mom. "Grandma, I don't want Rachel to go to Africa."

"But Rachel has to go. God called her and said, 'Rachel, I want you to go to Africa.'" Beth thought about that for a moment. Then she said, "How do we know He was talking about our Rachel? He might have meant some other Rachel." Then, summoning up all her reasoning powers, she asked a crucial question: "Did He use her first name and her last name?" Did He just say, "Rachel" or did He specify, "Rachel Jones"?

After all, there are a lot of Rachels in the world, and He could have meant someone else. The grandmother decided that this was such an important question that she and Beth called Rachel in California.

Rachel told Beth that God had indeed used her first name and her last name. Thus reassured, four-year-old Beth gave her blessing for Aunt Rachel to go to the mission field.

That, I think, is what Jesus meant when He said, "Unless you change and become like little children, you will never enter the kingdom of heaven" (Matt. 18:3). The faith that pleases God is childlike in its simplicity.

The word for *trust* in Hebrew means "to lean with the full body," "to lay upon," "to rest the full weight upon." To trust in the Lord is to rest your whole weight upon Him.

Trusting God isn't easy for many people. I'm thinking now of friends who moved from Chicago to a distant city. As the time drew near, the emotional stress of leaving the familiar for the unknown almost overwhelmed the wife.

Just before leaving, she made an interesting comment: "How did we get here? In my heart I believe we're doing the right thing, but looking back I'm not sure how we got from Point A to Point B. Only God could have done it, because I never would have done it myself." But she smiled when she said it.

Trusting God often involves great uncertainty and periods of deep doubt. But if you are willing to do what He wants you to do, He then takes responsibility to reach into the chaos of life and lead you step-by-step to the place He wants you to be.

Lord God, thank You for stepping into the confusion of my life and leading me forward. I still need Your help today. Amen.

1. What does the phrase "childlike faith" mean to you?
2. Do you find it hard to trust God right now?
3. Are you currently at "Point A" or "Point B" or somewhere in between?

WE'RE NOT IN HEAVEN YET

The Lord upholds all those who fall
and lifts up all who are bowed down.

PSALM 145:14

We're not finished yet—but we will be.

Perhaps you've heard the term "good enough for government work." That's a derisive (and somewhat unfair) way of saying, "Don't worry about the details. The joints don't have to fit, the margins can be crooked, and we don't need to worry about the budget. We don't have to be perfect; in fact, we don't even have to be close."

Mark it down plainly: God does not do shoddy work. Everything He does is perfect. But many of us feel like our lives are "government work." We look inside and see lots of good and bad mixed together and a whole bunch of loose connections and a lot of parts that don't seem to work right.

That's the way it is in a fallen world. We're stuck with what seems to be "government work" in this life. But it won't be that way forever. God has promised that in the end, we will be sanctified through and through.

We're not finished yet—but we will be.

We're not completely clean today—but we will be.

We're not wholly wise today—but we will be.

We're not totally redeemed right now—but we will be.

We're not always useful to God—but we will be.

John Calvin used a picturesque expression to describe what God is doing. God intends "the entire renovation of the man." I confess I never understood renovation until I moved to Oak Park, Illinois, in 1989. I soon learned what it means because everything in the village was under constant renovation. A "new" house was only seventy years old, and an average house was eighty-years old. An "old" house was at least a hundred years old.

Anyone who can renovate old buildings does a land office business in Oak Park. If you live in one of those houses, you never really get the job finished. First you work on the roof, then you start on the living room, then the kitchen, then the bedrooms one by one. Probably you'll have trouble with the plumbing and the electrical fixtures (more than once!).

Eventually you've got to replace the porch, repaint the trim, and install a new heater and maybe even an air conditioner. You can work on a house for fifteen years and still not be completely finished. There's always something else to do.

If you think houses are hard, try renovating a human life. That's a job so tough only God would attempt it. I think God just eventually says, "I've done all I can do down there. Come on up here and I'll finish the job where the working conditions are much better."

Today we are holy in spots. When God is finished with us, we will be holy through and through.

Holy Spirit, I long for the day when the renovation of my life will be complete. Until then, grant me faith to believe that the work continues even when I do not see it clearly. Amen.

1. If God intends the "entire renovation" of the redeemed person, why doesn't He do all of it the moment we are saved?
2. What are the advantages of gradual sanctification?
3. Name three places where your life is in need of extensive renovation.

CALLING ALL SAINTS

For the Lord takes delight in his people; he crowns the humble with salvation. Let the saints rejoice in this honor and sing for joy on their beds.

PSALM 149:4–5

Are you a saint?

Before you answer, let me give you a simple definition. The word *saint* simply means "holy one."

To many of us a "saint" refers to an extraordinary Christian, one who has been canonized by the Catholic Church. But the Bible never uses the word that way. It always applies to all believers.

I preach once a year at Word of Life Conference Center in Hudson, Florida. For the last few years, the same man has either picked us up or taken us back to the airport. I can't forget him because he always greets me the same way: "Hello, saint!" Not "Hello, Pastor Ray," but "Hello, saint!" He greets everyone that way.

He is Saint Harry to me. That's a perfectly biblical use of the world. I could speak of "Saint Jane" or "Saint Jeff" or "Saint Martha" or "Saint Don" or "Saint Fred." If you know Jesus, you are a true saint of God.

Many people think the word saint refers to a famous Christian, long dead, whose life was marked by exceptional piety. Thus, we speak of Saint Paul, Saint James, Saint

Christopher, Saint Jude, or Saint Nicholas. The implication being that they are saints, and we are not.

The truth of the matter is quite different. The Bible never uses the word *saint* to refer to a select group of super Christians. Rather, it was routinely applied in the New Testament to every Christian. This means every Christian is a saint of God. To put it another way, if you aren't a saint from the Bible's point of view, you're not a Christian at all.

A saint is a person who is holy. In some ways that seems like an odd description. Most of us probably don't feel very holy. We struggle with unholy thoughts and attitudes more than we would like to admit. But the Bible tells a different story. We who struggle so much with sin are called saints by God. Let that thought lift your spirits the next time you feel like a failure.

If you feel unworthy of sainthood, remember God does the choosing and He does it based on grace, not human merit. Rejoice in the honor of being called a saint of God.

When you go to bed tonight, sing for joy. It's amazing how far God will go to show us how much He loves us.

Lord God, thank You for numbering
me among Your saints—even when I am
very aware of being a sinner. Amen.

1. What do you think of when you hear the word *saint?*
2. How would you feel if someone called you a saint?
3. Complete this sentence: "My name is Saint ___________."
   Thank God for setting you apart to be holy.

WHO'S GOT IT BETTER THAN WE DO?

Let everything that has breath praise the Lord.

PSALM 150:6

It's time to praise the Lord!

Psalm 150 is packed with praise. The word *praise* occurs thirteen times.

- It tells us *where* to praise: in the sanctuary and in creation.
- It tells us *why* to praise: because of God's mighty power.
- It tells us *how* to praise: with music and dancing.
- It tells us *who* is to praise: anyone with a breath.

This is loud, exuberant, full-throated praise, using every instrument we have, to sing the praises of our God.

As I was finishing this book, I ran across a quote from Jarvis James: "If you have a pulse, you ought to have a praise." He's right. Are you breathing? Let everything that has breath praise the Lord. Is your heart beating? Then let it beat in praise to the Lord who has not forgotten you.

Perhaps you feel God has abandoned you. Perhaps you feel bitter because others have mistreated you. Maybe your sin has put you in a very bad place.

If so, remember this. God has not stopped showing

kindness to you. He wants your heart, and He will do whatever it takes to draw you to Him. He calls you by His grace, and He whispers through your pain, "My child, I have not forgotten you."

As I write these words, I am on Day 60 of 180 days of cancer treatment. The doctor says my outlook is good, but the Lord is the one who heals. As we were starting this journey, my wife said to me, "Honey, this is just the next step in God's plan for us."

Since then, we've started every day by praying for faith and gratitude, and for no grumbling. So far, the Lord has answered those prayers.

When Jim Harbaugh was coach of the Michigan Wolverines football team, he told a story that stuck in my mind. He said that as he and his brother John were growing up, whenever the family was going through a hard time, their father would say, "Who's got it better than we do?" And the boys would shout back, "No one!"

What a marvelous way to look at life. If you know Jesus, you have everything you need now and forever. Think of it. You are forgiven, redeemed, and indwelled by the Holy Spirit. You have new life now and someday you will spend eternity with Jesus in heaven.

God is our Father, the Lord Jesus is our Shepherd, and the Holy Spirit is our counselor. The Bible is our guide, the church is our home, and heaven is our destination. Jarvis James is right: "If you have a pulse, you ought to have a praise." Let everything that has breath praise the Lord!

Thank You, Lord, for Your gift of the book of Psalms. May my heart rejoice and my lips sing Your praise—now and forever! Amen.

1. Why are there so many different instruments listed in Psalm 150?
2. Name three reasons you can praise God right now.
3. One final question: Who's got it better than we do?

ACKNOWLEDGMENTS

This book was born 30 years ago.

Phyllis Raad, Sherrie Puknaitis, Rebecca Arellanes, Mia Gale, Kathy Duggins, and her daughters Sarah and Katie all contributed in various ways to the writing of this book. I gained many valuable insights from Craig Steiner, Larry Korbus, Bob Boerman, and Davis Duggins. Greg Thornton of Moody Publishers gave me constant encouragement, as did Julie-Allyson Ieron, Suzanne Dowd, Jim Bell, and Anne Scherich. I am also indebted to Sherry Crucifisso for her prayers.

Rob Teigen asked me to consider revising the book and publishing it with Christian Art Publishers. It's an honor to work with him and with the CAP team.

Special thanks to my wife Marlene for her careful reading of the earlier version. She made many wise suggestions on how to bring it up to date.

It has been an adventure to read what I wrote 30 years ago. I was a young man when I first wrote these words. Now that I am coming down the homestretch of life, I am more certain than ever that the fear of the Lord is the beginning of wisdom.

SPECIAL NOTE

If you would like to contact the author, you can reach him in the following ways:

By letter:

Ray Pritchard
P. O. Box 257
Elmhurst, IL 60126

By e-mail: ray@keepbelieving.com
Via the Internet: www.keepbelieving.com

ABOUT THE AUTHOR

Dr. Ray Pritchard serves as president of Keep Believing Ministries. He ministers extensively across the US and in South Korea, Ukraine, Uganda, Kenya, China, and the Philippines. He has written thirty-one books, including *Stealth Attack*, *The Healing Power of Forgiveness*, and *An Anchor for the Soul*. He is a co-host of "Today's Issues" on *American Family Radio*. He has been married to Marlene for 50 years. Their eleven grandchildren can be found in Kansas, Illinois, and Montana. Dr. Pritchard's hobbies include biking, surfing the Internet, and anything related to the Civil War. He recently hit the 50,000-mile mark on his bicycle riding.

ABOUT THE AUTHOR